OSPREY AIRCRAFT OF THE AC

# Finnish Aces
# of World War 2

SERIES EDITOR: TONY HOLMES

OSPREY AIRCRAFT OF THE ACES • 23

# Finnish Aces of World War 2

## Kari Stenman and Kalevi Keskinen

OSPREY
AVIATION

**Front cover**
On 6 March 1944 three Bf 109Gs of 1/HLeLv 34 and six Brewster Model 239s of 3/HLeLv 24 were sent to patrol the eastern end of the Gulf of Finland with the instruction to await the arrival of Soviet aircraft returning to their bases at Seiskari or Oranienbaum. At 1745, 16 Petlyakov Pe-2 bombers of 12.GBAP, escorted by a dozen fighters, were observed at a distance of one kilometre by the Finnish pilots. They immediately split up, with some fighters going for the bombers, and others for the escorts.

Attacking the Pe-2s, WO Ilmari Juutilainen had quickly shot two of them down and latched on to potentially his third kill when he saw two Bf 109s take position as his wingmen. Focusing once again on the fleeing bomber, Juutilainen was just about to open fire when his well-honed survival instincts told him to check his rear, where he spotted his 'Bf 109s' once again – although now they were Yak-7s! Realising that he had mistakenly identified his wingmen, he pulled hard on the control column and the Yaks shot by beneath him.

Choosing not to follow the startled Finn, they instead turning back to their base at Seiskari. In the meantime the Pe-2s had escaped, so Juutilainen chose to hunt down his would-be attackers. With the element of surprise on his side, he fired from close range with just his nose-mounted Rheinmetall-Borsig MG 17 machine guns following the jamming of the solitary 20 mm Mauser MG 151/20 cannon.

Finally alerted to the danger behind him, the Yak pilot attempted to evade the Finn's fire by banking away and then diving, but Juutilainen stuck grimly to his tail, shooting off short bursts as the pair descended to a height of just ten metres above the frozen sea. After a brief chase over the ice, the combat finally ended when the Soviet pilot hit the 'ground' and exploded.

The three kills scored by Ilmari Juutilainen on this sortie took his tally to 61, the last 17 of which had been claimed in Bf 109G-2 MT-222, featured in this specially-commissioned cover artwork by Iain Wyllie. WO Juutilainen ended the war as Finland's top ace with 94 confirmed and 34 unconfirmed aerial victories

First published in Great Britain in 1998 by Osprey Publishing, Elms Court, Chapel Way, Botley, Oxford OX2 9LP United Kingdom

© 1998 Osprey Publishing Limited

ISBN 1 85532 783 X

Edited by Tony Holmes
Page design by Tony Truscott
Cover Artwork by Iain Wyllie
Aircraft Profiles and Nose Art by Mark Styling
Figure Artwork by Mike Chappell
Scale Drawings by Mark Styling

Printed in Hong Kong

98 99 00 01 02   10 9 8 7 6 5 4 3 2 1

ACKNOWLEDGEMENTS
The authors wish to thank Carl-Fredrik Geust for providing details on Soviet units and operations, this information having sourced from original documents found in Russian archives that are kept in Moscow and St Petersburg

EDITOR'S NOTE
To make this best-selling series as authoritative as possible, the editor would be extremely interested in hearing from any individual who may have relevant photographs, documentation or first-hand experiences relating to the elite pilots, and their aircraft, of the various theatres of war. Any material used will be fully credited to its original source. Please write to Tony Holmes at 10 Prospect Road, Sevenoaks, Kent TN13 3UA United Kingdom.

FOR A CATALOGUE OF ALL BOOKS PUBLISHED BY OSPREY PLEASE WRITE TO:
The Marketing Manager, Osprey Publishing Ltd.,
P.O. Box 140, Wellingborough, Northants NN8 4ZA United Kingdom.

**Previous pages**
1/LeLv 34 pilots watch their colleagues performing aerobatics over Utti airfield on 1 June 1943. They are, from left to right, SSgt Eino Peltola, Sgt Lauri Mäittälä, 1Lt Lauri Pekuri and Sgt Erik Lyly (*ECPA*)

# CONTENTS

# WINTER WAR

In August 1939 Germany and the Soviet Union signed a non-aggression pact, much to the surprise of western nations. In a secret additional protocol to this agreement, found initially by the Americans after the war, and then again in documents discovered recently in Russia itself, the small independent Baltic states were annexed to the Molotov-von Ribbentrop pact, effectively allowing the Soviet Union to seize them upon the German invasion of Poland. One of those countries unwittingly affected by this secret annexation was Finland.

Germany launched its attack on Poland on 1 September 1939, and within three weeks had gained control of the western parts of the country (see *Aircraft of the Aces 21 - Polish Aces of World War 2* for further details). As agreed in the non-aggression pact, the Soviet Union occupied the eastern provinces of Poland, whilst at the same time forcibly demanding access to air and naval bases within the Baltic countries.

Only Finland remained defiant in the face of communist threats, and while the Red Army overtly massed troops on the eastern border of the Soviet Union in an attempt to scare the Finns into submission, negotiations continued in Moscow between politicians from the two countries. The Soviets wanted large areas of Karelia (which included numerous military establishments) handed over in return for barren land given to Finland in the northern wilderness. All communist overtures were disguised under the 'the safety of Leningrad' banner, which the Finns correctly sus-

Lightly camouflaged Fokker D.XXI FR-86 of 2/LLv 24 (the second Flight of *Lentolaivue* 24) is seen at Utti on 1 December 1939 – the second day of the Winter War. 2/LLv 24's flight leader, 1Lt Jaakko Vuorela, claimed his squadron's first aerial victory in this very fighter on this day when he downed a Tupolev SB bomber of 24.SBAP (fast bomber aviation regiment) over the Karelian Isthmus. As this shot reveals, the first real winter's snow had just started falling, and within a week skis had been fitted to all the Fokker fighters (*SA-kuva*)

LLv 32 D.XXI FR-92 is seen in flight some months after the Winter War had ended. Photographed over Siikakangas in August 1940, this machine still wears the tactical markings applied by 4/LLv 24 some six months earlier. During the winter conflict it was regularly flown by deputy flight leader 1Lt 'Pelle' Sovelius, who used it to score six kills (*Ilmailu*)

pected was a cover for the total conquest of their country – recent research in Russia has revealed a detailed plan which backs these suspicions up. Suspecting the worst, the Finnish armed forces carried out a full-scale mobilisation whilst the negotiations continued.

Throughout the build up to war, Finland (perhaps naively) trusted in its neutral status being recognised through its membership of the League of Nations, and so said 'no' to all proposals insulting its sovereignty. The USSR broke off negotiations following receipt of this answer on 28 November 1939, annulled the 1932 non-aggression pact between the two nations, and attacked 48 hours later. The Winter War had started.

## FIGHTER DEFENCES

In 1937 the Finnish Air Force issued a five-year development plan which called primarily for the acquisition of 'interceptors'. It was correctly deduced that any enemy attacking Finland would rely heavily on the large-scale use of bombers, without fighter escort. With only limited funds available, the Finns would have to procure these interceptors from sources other than the major European powers, who could not spare military aircraft in the growing climate of political tension.

Eventually, the Finns struck a deal with Dutch company Fokker that saw them purchase seven D.XXIs outright, and an assembly license for a further 35 examples As a result of being turned down by all major manufacturers, the Finnish Air Force had only received two-thirds of its new interceptors when the Red Army attacked. On 30 November 1939 some 36 D.XXIs were available for combat, these being divided between three flights in *Lentolaivue* (LLv) 24 and two in *Lentolaivue* 26, all of which were under the command of LLv's 24 Capt Gustaf Erik Magnusson.

The remainder of the fighter force consisted of ten obsolete Bristol Bulldog IVAs in LLv 26's third flight, their use being limited to the defence of areas to the rear of the frontline and vulnerable towns and ports. Both LLvs 24 and 26 were part of *Lentorykmentti* 2, commanded by creator of the Finnish fighter arm, Lt Col Richard Lorentz.

According to Soviet sources, there were 3253 aircraft deployed to the

Seen wearing full flying gear, 1Lt Per-Erik Sovelius poses near the tail of FR-92 in January 1940. The veteran ace later headed Brewster-equipped 4/LeLv 24 during the Continuation War

4/LLv 24 pilots are seen in front of D.XXI FR-110 in January 1940 – group shots like this one were rarely taken during the Winter War, as the outside temperature at this time of year was typically -35°C. The pilots visible in this shot are, from left to right, Sgt Martti Alho, 2Lt Tapani Harmaja, 1Lt Jussi Räty, 1Lt Veikko Karu, Maj Gustaf Magnusson, WO Viktor Pyötsiä, MSgt Sakari Ikonen, 1Lt Per-Erik Sovelius, 2Lt Iikka Törrönen and an unidentified war correspondent. With the exception of Harmaja and Räty, all these men later became aces (*J Sarvanto*)

Finnish front, which stretched from the Gulf of Finland to the Arctic Sea. The bulk of these were concentrated on the Karelian Isthmus, which would become the key frontline of the Winter War. This formidable armada would fly an average of 1000 sorties per day.

## FIGHTER TACTICS

Despite their paucity in numbers, Finnish fighter pilots were highly trained individuals who had been well indoctrinated in modern tactics by Richard Lorentz. As early as 1934, then Maj Lorentz had discovered (flying Gamecocks at LLv 24) that the traditional fighter formation of a lead aircraft and two wingmen was less suited to aerial combat than was a pair of aircraft. The latter could adopt a more flexible approach to engaging an enemy due to their being one less aircraft involved, and their numbers could be increased when the need arose through the addition of a second pair, thus creating what the Luftwaffe dubbed a *Schwarm*.

Before assuming the command of LLv 24, Magnusson made visits to a number of other air forces which included included a three-month 'tour' with newly-created JG 132 'Richthofen'. As previously mentioned, the Germans had also given up the three-aircraft formation in favour of the 'finger four'. This convinced the Finnish 'top brass' that the newly adopted basic formations were right, and that the tactics developed around them were sound.

Lack of funding for the Finnish Air Force of the 1930s not only affected its equipment levels but also pilot training. Therefore, a student destined for fighters would receive elementary flying training but no advanced tuition. This effectively meant that he was taught two, or maybe three, methods of attacking enemy aircraft, but no more. This was based on the discovery that a bomber could usually be brought

5/LLv 24 D.XXI FR-105 is seen at Joroinen in April 1940. During the Winter War future aces Sgts Lasse Aaltonen and Onni Paronen (then both members of LLv 26) scored victories in this particular fighter. The fitment of skis in place of wheels on the Fokker's fixed undercarriage legs had very little effect on the fighter's performance

down with two (or three at most) passes. These three methods, and associated gunnery, were rehearsed both in training and with the front-line units, and they served both doctrinal and economical limits.

To achieve success in three passes, guns were set to converge at 150 m, but pilots were trained not to fire until at 50 m distance. Closing to this proximity was a risky undertaking, but being that close to the bomber gave them two advantages: 1) they were immune to defensive fire, and 2) they could not miss.

When war broke out, Magnusson gave strict orders to avoid fighter duels, for the D.XXI lacked the manoeuvrability to turn with the Soviet Polikarpov I-15bis, I-16s and I-153s. However, it was more than suited to the role of bomber interceptor, and even if lacking outright speed, it had a good rate of climb and could always be pulled away in a dive.

4/LLv 24's 1Lt Jorma 'Zamba' Sarvanto has good reason to be smiling, for whilst flying this very fighter (D.XXI FR97) on 6 January 1940 he downed six DB-3 bombers in just four minutes. Like most other Finnish aces, he latter saw action in Brewsters, scoring four victories to raise his final tally to 17 in 251 missions (*J Sarvanto*)

## FIRST ENCOUNTERS

30 November 1939 was a cloudy day, and on the few interception missions flown no enemy aircraft were met. Next morning, the Red Air Forces sent out a wave of around 250 aircraft to bomb Helsinki and other ports, a second formation to attack the airfields in south-eastern Finland and fighters to patrol midway along Karelian Isthmus.

Despite being comprehensively outnumbered, the Finnish fighter pilots were ready to repel the bombers, having been mobilised some weeks before. The first contact was made at 1145 when two Bulldogs were jumped by six I-16s of 7.IAP (fighter aviation regiment). The Finnish pilots were immediately separated from each other, and SSgt Uuttu (flying BU-64) was left alone to fight the Russians. After scoring hits on a 'Rata', he himself was shot down, crashing at Muolaanjärvi and suffering injuries in the process. Uuttu's I-16 also came down, however, thus becoming the first aerial victory scored over Finland.

Soon after this initial engagement, LLv 24 scrambled D.XXIs in pairs, led by Capt Magnusson (in his regular FR-99). Between noon and 1500 the unit completed 59 sorties, destroying eight Tupolev SB bombers from 41.SBAP (fast bomber aviation regiment) and three from 24.SBAP between Lappeenranta and Seivästö. 1Lt Vuorela claimed two victories, while Capt Magnusson, 1Lt Ahola, 1Lt Luukkanen, 1Lt Räty, 2Lt Kokko and Sgts Heikinaro, Nissinen, Rautakorpi and Virta each got one apiece.

Poor weather and snow fall then stopped all flying until 19 December, when LLv 24 flew 58 sorties over the Karelian Isthmus and engaged in combat on 22 occasions between 1050 and 1520 hours. The Soviets lost seven SBs (six from 44.SBAP) and five Ilyushin DB-3s from other regiments. SSgt Virta (in FR-84) was the first Finnish pilot to engage the enemy on this day, although he encountered 25.IAP I-16 fighters rather than bombers. Nevertheless, he quickly destroyed two of his opponents.

Four days later the luckless 44.SBAP was again attacked by the Fokkers, losing six SBs over the Karelian Isthmus at 1100 – 1Lt Sarvanto claimed

Seen at the Immola officers' mess 24 hours after his astounding 7 January 1940 clash with the Soviet air force, 1Lt Sarvanto shows off the crumpled rudder fabric taken from one of the six 6.DBAP (long-range aviation regiment) DB-3M bombers that he had shot down with just 2000 rounds of machine-gun fire (*SA-kuva*)

Another Winter War survivor, FR-116 of 5/LLv 24 sits at Joroinen on 8 April 1940. Although barely visible on the original print of this photograph, there is a blue '4' painted on the rudder of FR-116, denoting its allocation to the 5th flight. Along with the 1st flight, 5/LLv 24 was manned by LLv 26 pilots until they returned to their original unit on 1 February 1940

Seen on page eight forming the backdrop for the group shot of 4/LLv 24 pilots, FR-110 looks a little worse for wear in this 8 April 1940 view after its pilot had effected a forced landing at Joroinen following the the loss of the aircraft's port ski in flight – it was assigned to 3/LLv 24 at the time. WO Viktor Pyötsiä had flown this aircraft with notable success during the conflict, claiming 7.5 victories with it. FR-110 is the only LLv 24 D.XXI to have been photographed bearing victory markings, these taking the form of four and a half vertical bars on the fighter's fin

two in FR-97. Some 21 engagements were fought on this date, and aside from the bombers, two I-16s from both 7.IAP and 64.IAP were also downed – Sgt Tilli, flying FR-103, accounted for the former pair.

LLv 24 scored steadily throughout their first month of operations, downing an incredible 54 aircraft for the loss of just one Fokker destroyed and another damaged. On the ground, Finnish troops were also enjoying similar successes disproportionate to their numbers, having effectively halted the Soviet advances in all directions.

## 6 JANUARY 1940

During the morning of 6 January, 17 DB-3Ms of 6.DBAP (long-range bomber aviation regiment) took off in two waves from Estonia to bomb Kuopio, in eastern Finland. The first nine Ilyushins attacked their target as planned, but the second formation of eight drifted too far west and crossed the Gulf of Finland south of Utti. Based nearby was 4/LLv 24, who had 1Lt Sovelius (in FR-92) up on patrol. He attacked the DB-3Ms at 1010 at 3000 m, downing the outer aircraft at the left of the formation.

The remaining seven bombers continued to Kuopio, where they released their bombs to little effect before returning home along the same route, which followed a railway line. 1Lt Sarvanto had, meanwhile, taken off in order meet the DB-3s on their return journey, and in his postwar memoirs, he describes the famous four-minute battle which ensued;

'The clouds over Utti had disappeared and the sun gleamed from the light bellies of the marvellous looking row of bombers. I counted them to be seven. On the left flew an echelon of three and to the right four almost in a row. The distance between the planes was hardly one aircraft.

'I banked to the right and headed south, continuing to climb. For a moment I was in the sights of the nose gunners, but facing the sun, they obviously did not see me. When I reached the altitude of the bombers, I was already 500 m behind them. At full power, I started the chase and selected the one at the extreme left of the formation, although the bomber third from the left was further behind the others, and the fire from its rear gunner felt dangerous. At a distance of 300 m it banged unpleasantly into my plane – I had flown into a stream of bullets.

'I opened fire at 20 m with a short burst to the fuselage of the machine on the left. The tracers seemed to hit the target, and I quickly silenced the bomber's rear gunner. I took aim again at the right engines of both

bombers in formation, and with light touches on the trigger, both enemies went down in flames. I cheered, and then aligned my Fokker up with the bombers on the opposite side of the formation. Attacking as I had before, I set the engines of one bomber alight, before turning to the next aircraft in the formation, hitting it with gun fire at a very close range. This planes too burst into flames soon after I had hit it with two or three very short bursts. On the right I saw the first aircraft that I had attacked on this side of the formation diving as a fireball towards the ground.

'I now set myself the goal of destroying all the remaining bombers in the formation. Some fell away like burning pages of a book after I had fired at them, whilst others pulled up steeply following the incapacitation of their pilot. The reddish January sun shone through the haze towards me throughout the engagement, except when the dark smoke of the burning planes cast a shadow across it.

'The penultimate bomber was much tougher than the others to shoot down, for my wing guns were probably empty by then. It did, however, finally catch fire, and I in turn went after the last one. Its rear gunner had been silent for quite some time, and I went in very close. I aimed at the engine and pulled the trigger. The guns were quiet! I made a couple of charging attempts but without any result. I had ran out of ammunition, and the only thing to do was to return home.'

Despite this, Sarvanto had inflicted enough damage on six of the DB-3s to ensure that they crashed between Utti and Tavastila – a distance of 30 kms. He thus became Finland's premier ace in an action that lasted just four minutes. His D.XXI (FR-97) had received 23 hits, although none were serious, and it was flown to the repair facility. Once news of the action was released, foreign pressmen showed much interest in Sarvanto, for nothing like this had occurred in Europe up to this point in the war.

On 17 January ten DXXIs scrambled at 1355 hours and caught three formations of SBs (25 aircraft in total) from 54.SBAP returning from a raid via the Karelian Isthmus. Twenty-five minutes later, nine bombers had met their end, and several more were damaged.

Two days later both 1Lt Nieminen, flying FR-78, and SSgt Virta in FR-84 became the next aces by downing an SB each over the Karelian Isthmus. Following these reversals, Soviet bombers avoided the airspace over south-eastern Finland for almost two weeks. Other regions were still experiencing bomber activity, however, and on 20 January 1Lt Luukkanen led the interception of SBs from 21.DBAP north of Lake Ladoga. They succeeded in destroying five bombers, with WO Pyötsiä (in FR-110) scoring two and SSgt Tilli (in FR-107) one to both become aces.

## FLYGFLOTTILJ 19

Although performing well in the Karelian Isthmus region, the Finns had no aircraft spare to protect their barren northern border. Fortunately for them, however, Sweden was worried about its own position should Finland fall, and duly assembled a voluntary unit containing both infantry and air detachments. It was quickly deployed to Lapland upon its arrival in Finland, and on 10 January the flying unit, designated *Flygflottilj* 19 (comprising 12 Gladiators and four Harts), arrived at Kemi and was stationed on the ice outside Veitsiluoto. This small detachment then represented one-third of Sweden's total fighter force.

Two days later F 19 flew its first mission when Harts attacked 145.IAP's base at Märkäjärvi whilst Gladiators provided top cover. Bad luck struck during the return flight, however, when two Harts collided and one was downed by fighters. 2Lt Iacobi, in Gladiator 'F', managed to destroy one of the attacking I-15bis for the first Swedish aerial victory.

F 19 served till the end of hostilities, and although it claimed only eight aircraft downed during 600 sorties, its presence in Lapland effectively prevented the bombings of towns in the northern region.

1/LLv 24 pilot WO Yrjö Turkka flew FR-83 during the Winter War, scoring four-and-a-half victories with it. The machine is seen here at Siikakangas in the summer of 1940 still bearing Turkka's 'black 2' markings, despite having been transferred to LLv 32

## TEST PILOTS AT WAR

Finland's State Aircraft Factory was located at Tampere in the southern central region of the country, and the airfield at this site was shared with the air force's *Koelentue* (KoeL - Testflight). Pilots assigned to this unit carried out acceptance flights on new or repaired aircraft leaving the factory, which became a prime target following the outbreak of war.

On 13 January 1940, KoeL leader, Capt Ehrnrooth, scored the first kill to fall to the test pilots whilst flying Fiat G.50 SA-1. He destroyed an SB bomber south-east of Tampere, and two days later another SB fell to the guns of a Fokker on a check flight following repairs.

As mentioned previously in this chapter, 20 January 1940 proved to be a costly day for the Russians, with 35.SBAP in particular suffering major losses. Six of its SBs were downed by three LLv 24 D.XXIs scrambled to intercept them, four falling to the guns of FR-91, flown by 1Lt Itävuori. Later that same day the high-scoring Fokker was again in action when LLv 24 pilot 1Lt Huhanantti bounced three SBs of 36.SBAP whilst attempting to rendezvous with the rest of his unit. He quickly destroyed two bombers before wisely breaking off when five I-153s appeared on the scene. The latter aircraft were now equipped with drop tanks, which allowed them to patrol in large formations over southern Finland.

The final KoeL kill came on 2 March 1940, taking their tally to nine victories. On that same day the unit's only loss occurred when WO Heiskala, piloting FR-84, was downed by a DB-3 gunner.

Yet another LLv 32 D.XXI, FR-108 is run up at Siikakangas during the summer of 1940. 3/LLv 24 leader Capt Eino Luukkanen had flown this aircraft ('blue and white 6') during the previous winter's conflict, claiming one Soviet aircraft solely destroyed and another shared

### FOREIGN HELP ARRIVES

Aside from the Fokker fighters purchased by the Finns, an order for 25 Fiat G.50s for LLv 26 was also placed with the Italian manufacturer on 23 October 1939. To ensure their speedy arrival in Finland, the initial delivery route for

these aircraft called for them to be sent by rail through Germany and then across the Baltic Sea by ship to Sweden, where they would be assembled and flown to Finland. Two aircraft arrived via this route in late December 1939, and six more had reached the German port of Stettin, on the Baltic Sea, before the Germans turned them back to Switzerland. These G.50s, plus the remaining aircraft, were then sent by sea from Italy, causing their arrival to be delayed until 15 February 1940.

Soon after the Soviet invasion, the British government donated 30 Gladiator IIs to the Finns, and the first of these arrived on 18 January – others followed four weeks later. LLv 26 was thus temporarily equipped with the Gloster fighter until 1 March, when they were handed over to *Lentorykmentti* 1's LLv 12 and 14.

New units were also formed to operate these foreign 'donor' aircraft, although when LLv 28 was created on 8 December 1939, its pilot had no idea what aircraft they would be fly. Then at the beginning of 1940 France donated 50 Morane-Saulnier MS.406 fighters, which were duly issued to the unit. Again, their delivery took place by sea to Sweden, where Swedes and Finns worked side-by-side assembling the aircraft. The first French fighters arrived in Finland on 4 February and went straight to the unit, and by the end of the month some 30 had been flown in.

A hectic attempt to purchase America fighters led, on 16 December 1939, to a deal that saw the Finns buy 44 Brewster Model 239s at a competitive price. These aircraft had originally been intended for the US Navy, but Brewster had sold the latter customer improved F2A-2s instead. Delivery of the now surplus Model 239s took place by sea, with assembly in Sweden – six arrived on 13 March, just prior to the end of the Winter War. These aircraft were issued to the new LLv 22.

Also arriving too late to see action were ten (of twelve) ex-RAF Hurricane Is bought from Britain, which flew in during the second week of March. France also 'gifted' 80 surplus Caudron-Renault CR.714 Cyclone lightweight fighters to the Finns, six arriving soon after the war. Fortunately, no more were received, as due to the type's poor landing and take-off characteristics, they were immediately grounded – permanently.

Following a period of stalemate on the frontline, the Soviet forces launched the second phase of their offensive on the Karelian Isthmus on 1 February. Red Army assets poured into the battlefield from other fronts in an effort to force a breakthrough, whilst the bombers switched from strategic targets to tactical support of the offensive and large fighter formations patrolled both the battlefield and into Finnish territory.

During this time the number of serviceable Finnish fighters rose from 45 to 67, with the Gladiators tackling the fighters and the D.XXI continuing to intercept bomber formations – the latter mission now grew steadily more difficult with the introduction of a fighter escorts.

After two weeks of familiarisation flying with the Gladiator, LLv 26 scored its first kills on 2 February 1940 when 1Lt Berg engaged six I-153s of OIAE (a detached fighter aviation *escadrille*), downing one near his base. Later that same day SSgt Tuominen (in GL-258) chased two SBs and six I-16s over the Gulf of Finland, downing one fighter over Kotka and another near the island of Suursaari.

Eleven days later, whilst six Gladiators tangled with I-153s north of Lake Ladoga, nine SBs of 39.SBAP arrived in the midst of the dogfight

just as WO Lautamäki and his wingman (SSgt Tuominen) joined the
battle. With the escorts busy fighting the bulk of LLv 26, the two
Finns attacked the bombers without
interference and shot five of them in
quick succession. Tuominen's share
was three-and-a-half in GL-255,
which made him the first Gladiator
ace. His squadronmates then
attacked the bombers and claimed
another two destroyed.

Based in south-western Finland in order to protect vital ports, LLv 28
also went into battle with little more than two weeks' experience on their
Moranes. On 17 February they drew 'first blood' by sending a DB-3
down over the south-western archipelago. Three days later 1Lt Berg
became the second Gladiator ace when he used GL-280 to attack 30 SBs
of 6.DBAP sent to bomb Kouvola. Although he destroyed one of the
Tupolevs, Berg was in turn burnt whilst bailing out of his blazing fighter,
which had been hit by defensive fire from the remaining bombers.

The aerial battles over the Karelian Isthmus on 25 February were some
of the fiercest of the war, causing casualties on both sides. LLv 26 was in
the thick of the action, sending three Gladiators to drive off nine R-5
artillery fire-control aircraft, escorted by six I-153s from 13.OIAE. After
downing four 'spotting' aircraft, two Gladiators were in turn lost and a
third damaged in a forced landing following combat with the I-153s.

This engagement confirmed that LLv 26's Gladiators were finding it
increasingly difficult to fend off Soviet I-16s and I-153s, so after just ten
days of training on the Fiat G.50, the unit was thrust into combat with the
Italian fighter. On 26 February 1Lt Puhakka, leading a formation of three
G.50s sent to intercept fighters and bombers south of Kouvola, shot
down an I-16 flying FA-4, whilst his wingman, 2Lt Linnamaa, destroyed
a DB-3.

The Finns suffered further losses on the 29th when Soviet fighters carried out a series of raids on the bases of LLv 24 and 26. At Ruokolahti,
49.IAP fighters also downed a Gladiator in the morning. At noon,
'bombers' were supposedly detected approaching Ruokolahti, but these
instead turned out to be six I-153 'Chaikas' and 18 I-16 'Ratas' from
68.IAP. The Gladiators that were
scrambled to intercept the raiders
were caught just as they commenced
their take-off, and three were
instantly destroyed. A further two
Gloster fighters and a single D.XXI
were subsequently lost in the low-
altitude combat which followed,
although an I-16 was also downed
and another crashed into trees.

By March the Finnish army had
withdrawn from the Karelian Isthmus, although it remained steadfast

*Lentolaivue* **Fiat G.50 FA-26 is seen on a visit to Kauhava on 27 July 1940. This aircraft was later assigned to Oiva Tuominen, who used it to destroy 13 aircraft whilst part of 1/LeLv 26 (*Finnish Air Force*)**

in front of Viipuri. Sensing retreat, the Red Army commenced crossing the frozen Gulf of Finland west of Viipuri on the 2nd.

Soviet forces soon established two small bridgeheads on the mainland, and in order prevent a full-scale invasion, the entire Finnish air force was sent into action against troops, tanks and supply columns crossing the ice. The air force went about its task with clinical precision, light and medium bombers stopping the motorised units in their tracks and fighters strafing the infantry. The Red Army was were caught totally exposed on the vast open spaces of the icefield, and within a week the invasion had been suppressed. Theses sorties also attracted Soviet fighters into the area, and after myriad combats, both sides had lost five aircraft apiece.

The situation on the Karelian Isthmus was still critical when peace negotiations commenced in Moscow on 8 March. The resistance of the Finnish forces, supported by material help from western nations who threatened to join in militarily if the invasion continued, convinced the USSR that further action would only see the war expand into an international crisis, which they did not want. So, on 13 March at 1100 hours a cease-fire commenced. Accordingly, but unjustifiably, Finland handed over those tracts of land that the Soviets had demanded back in late 1939.

*Lentorykmentti* 2 fighters had flown 3486 sorties, claimed 170 aircraft shot down (and another 70 damaged) and produced ten aces, all for the and loss of 23 fighters in action. In all, the Finnish Air Force flew 5693 sorties and claimed 207 aircraft destroyed for the loss of 53 of their own on operations. Anti-aircraft guns also destroyed a further 314 aircraft.

Soviet air forces had flown 100,970 sorties over the Finnish front, claiming 427 aerial victories for the loss of 261 aircraft according to contemporary Soviet records. However, recent research of Russian archives has indicated that Soviet losses amounted to 579 aircraft, which is a figure well in line with total Finnish claims of 521.

## Winter War Aces

| Rank | Name | Squadron | Victories |
| --- | --- | --- | --- |
| 1Lt | Sarvanto, Jorma | 24 | 13 |
| SSgt | Tuominen, Oiva | 26 | 8 |
| WO | Pyötsiä, Viktor | 24 | 7.5 |
| 1Lt | Huhanantti, Tatu | 24 | 6 |
| 1Lt | Nieminen, Urho | 26 | 6 |
| 1Lt | Puhakka, Olli | 26 | 6 |
| MSgt | Virta, Kelpo | 24 | 6 |
| 1Lt | Sovelius Per-Erik | 24 | 5.5 |
| SSgt | Tilli, Pentti | 26 | 5 |
| 1Lt | Berg, Paavo | 26 | 5 |

# FINNISH OFFENSIVE OF 1941

**W**ith new fighters having been received from abroad, and many more still on their way to Finland, the air force decided to re-organise itself just a fortnight after the Winter War had ended. On 27 March 1940 *Lentorykmentti* 3 was duly established, this second fighter regiment controlling three units – namely LLv 30, which received Gloster Gauntlets donated by South Africa, LLv 32 (ex-LLv 22), whose Brewsters were exchanged with LLv 24's D.XXIs within three weeks of its formation, and LLv 34, which flew an array of advanced trainers.

*Lentorykmentti* 2 remained unchanged, however, LLv 24 retaining its Brewsters, LLv 26 Fiat G.50s and LLv 28 MS.406s. New bases were also built and the fighter pilot training programme totally overhauled.

Following the German occupation of Denmark and Norway in April 1940, and then the Benelux countries and France just two months later, Finland became geopolitically isolated, sandwiched between a previous enemy to the east and Germany to the west. When the latter country approached the Finns in August 1940 to see if they would be interested in acquiring captured war material in return for the transit of German troops bound for northern Norway, an agreement was soon reached.

This deal provided the air force with 25 ex-French MS.406s and 29 Curtiss Hawk 75As from ex-French and Norwegian stocks, the majority of which had arrived in time to see action in the new conflict.

The State Aircraft Factory also assembled 50 Twin Wasp Junior-powered D.XXIs, plus repaired enough captured aircraft from the Winter War to equip one entire fighter flight with I-153s!

## PRELUDE TO WAR

The German surprise attack on the USSR, codenamed Operation *Barbarossa*, was revealed to Finnish military leaders four weeks before it commenced on 22 June 1941. Armed with this knowledge, the Finns instigated a full-scale mobilisation four days prior to the invasion

'Father' of the modern Finnish fighter force, Maj Gustaf Magnusson commanded LeLv 24 until the end of May 1943. He is seen here in his Brewster at the start of the Finnish offensive to Karelia on 10 July 1941. Magnusson was both a great leader and teacher, and both attributes duly earned him the Mannerheim Cross on 26 June 1944 – he was CO of LeR 3 at the time (*SA-kuva*)

Soon after the commencement of *Barbarossa*, Soviet intelligence discovered a large number of German aircraft based on Finnish airfields, which made the communists fearful of a massive air raid launched on Leningrad from this direction. On the Finnish front, which stretched from the Gulf of Finland to the Arctic Sea, the Red air forces were equipped with 224 fighters and 263 bombers, and early on the morning of 25 June 1941, about 150 of the latter took off and attacked several locations in southern Finland. So began the Continuation War.

The Finnish fighter force was now in much better shape than it had been some 17 months before, as the following table shows:

| *Lentorykmentti 2* | **Lt Col R Lorenz** | **Pieksämäki** | |
|---|---|---|---|
| E/LeLv 24 | Maj G Magnusson | Vesivehmaa | |
| 1/LeLv 24 | Capt E Luukkanen | Vesivehmaa | 9 BW |
| 2/LeLv 24 | Capt L. Ahola | Selänpää | 8 BW |
| 3/LeLv 24 | 1Lt J Karhunen | Vesivehmaa | 8 BW |
| 4/LeLv 24 | 1Lt P-E Sovelius | Vesivehmaa | 8 BW |
| | | | |
| E/LeLv 26 | Maj R Harju-Jeanty | Joroinen | |
| 1/LeLv 26 | 1Lt M Linkola | Joroinen | 7 FA |
| 2/LeLv 26 | Capt E Kivinen | Joroinen | 9 FA |
| 3/LeLv 26 | 1Lt U Nieminen | Joroinen | 10 FA |
| | | | |
| E/LeLv 28 | Capt S-E Siren | Naarajärvi | |
| 1/LeLv 28 | Capt T Tanskanen | Naarajärvi | 7 MS |
| 2/LeLv 28 | 1Lt R Turkki | Naarajärvi | 10 MS |
| 3/LeLv 28 | 1Lt E Lupari | Naarajärvi | 10 MS |
| | | | |
| *Lentorykmentti 3* | **Lt Col E Nuotio** | **Pori** | |
| E/LeLv 30 | Capt L Bremer | Pori | |
| 1/LeLv 30 | Capt H Kalaja | Hollola | 5 HC |
| 2/LeLv 30 | 1Lt V Karu | Pori | 12 FRw |
| 3/LeLv 30 | 1Lt E Ilveskorpi | Pori | 6 FRw |
| | | | |
| E/LeLv 32 | Capt E Heinilä | Hyvinkää | |
| 1/LeLv 32 | Capt P Berg | Hyvinkää | 6 FRm |
| 2/LeLv 32 | Capt K Lahtela | Hyvinkää | 6 FRm |
| | | | |
| *Lentolaivue 6* | **Maj K Ilanko** | **Turku** | |
| 3/LeLv 6 | Capt L Karjalainen | Turku | 5 VH |

## 25 JUNE 1941

The large bomber formations heading for southern Finland were first spotted at 0700, and the news was quickly relayed t to Selänpää, where Maj Magnusson had forward deployed 2/LeLv 24 in anticipation of just such an air raid. At 0710 two Brewsters were scrambled, with SSgt Kinnunen flying BW-352 and Cpl Lampi BW-354. The latter pilot engaged the enemy first, and he described his engagement in the following report;

'Five minutes after take-off I noticed a large enemy formation. I attacked the plane on the extreme right and set it alight with my first

Maj Magnusson's Model 239 BW-380 is seen at Rantasalmi in July 1941, soon after he had used it to 'make ace' on the 8th. Flying a total of 158 missions, he downed five bombers and shared in a sixth kill

3/LeLv 26 pilots relive the 25 June 1941 battle over Joroinen, during which they destroyed 10 out of 15 72.SBAP bombers encountered. From the left they are 2Lt Carl-Erik Bruun, Sgt Ilmari Pöysti, 1Lt Urho Nieminen, SSgt Onni Paronen, 2Lt Sakari Kokkonen, 1Lt Olli Puhakka and MSgt Valio Porvari (*SA-kuva*)

burst. The aircraft went in a vertical dive and crashed into the forest. I then shot at two bombers on the right-hand side of a three-aircraft echelon, and they both began to smoke. I then attacked the remaining aircraft in the echelon. It too started to smoke and dived to the surface, but remained in the air. I gave chase and the enemy suddenly slowed, forcing me to pull up alongside him. At this point the rear gunner hit me from very close range.

'I pulled up and banked again behind the bomber, firing a short burst into it which created a fire on its right side. It subsequently hit the water burning. I saw SSgt Kinnunen also down two aircraft in the same battle.'

The Finnish pilots had engaged 27 SBs from 201.SBAP at 1500 m as they approached Heinola, the Soviets losing five bombers in total. Kinnunen and Lampi were both credited with two-and-a-half bombers apiece, with the former pilot becoming an ace on this sortie, since he had previously scored 3.5 kills during the Winter War.

Further interceptions later that morning saw the Brewster pilots destroy five more SBs, with WO Turkka (in BW-351) downing two to add to his score of 4.5 from the Winter War. SSgt Kinnunen also claimed two during his second sortie of the day, raising his tally to 4.5.

Recent research has shown that ten SB bombers (three from 2.SBAP,

3/LeLv 26 flight leader 1Lt Nieminen is congratulated by his mechanic Erkki Haimi while Petteri Markkanen looks on. The pilot had used FA-11 (seen behind him) to down a trio of SB bombers on 25 June 1941, three small bars denoting this achievement being visible at the base of the rudder

2/LeLv 26 pilot MSgt Lasse Aaltonen poses in front of a Fiat G.50 at Joroinen at the beginning of the Continuation War. On 25 June 1941 he had become an ace whilst flying FA-33 when he claimed 1.5 SB bombers destroyed, these successes adding to his tally of four Winter War victories. He is seen here wearing an Italian Salvatore parachute

Mechanics R Ranta and H Luukkonen stand in front of Aaltonen's FA-35 at Joroinen on 28 June 1941. All of 2/LeLv 26's Fiats carried a black and yellow tactical number on the tail, and this G.50 is no exception. Aaltonen went on to fly Bf 109Gs with 3/HLeLv 34 later in the war, raising his tally to 12.5 victories during 300 missions

SSgt Eero Kinnunen poses for official photographers at Selänpää on 25 June 1941. He had just destroyed 4.5 SB bombers on two missions flying 2/LeLv 24 machine BW-352 (seen behind him). Like Lasse Aaltonen, Kinnunen had also enjoyed success during the Winter War, claiming 3.5 kills (SA-kuva)

six from 201.SBAP and one from 202.SBAP) were lost in LeLv 24's operational area that day, which matches the figure claimed by the Brewster pilots. LeLv 32, based at Hyvinkää, engaged the enemy next, 1Lt Evinen (in D.XXI FR-116) leading his *Schwarm* southwards at 0800 to intercept 'DB-3s' returning to the USSR via Helsinki – his unit downed two. These aircraft were actually SBs from 4.SAD (mixed aviation division).

As the third unit to see action on the 25th, LeLv 26 had been flying air combat patrols all morning. Its 2nd Flight had just landed when 15 SBs of 72.SBAP attacked Joroinen at 1145 from 1000 m. Despite being low on fuel, two Fiats took off amidst the falling bombs and caught the attackers, sending three down.

Meanwhile, 1Lt Nieminen, who had led the six G.50s of 3/LeLv 26 straight passed the bombers without spotting them, was immediately called back to his base by radio. Diving on the bombers from a superior height at 1155, the Fiat pilots destroyed 10 bombers in just 20 minutes. Nieminen described the melee in the following report;

'My flight engaged a 15-20 aircraft formation of SBs above Tuuksjärvi. I hit two aircraft on the right side of the formation, and both had their engines set alight. Over Kerisalo island I managed to get into a good position behind a third SB. Its fuel tank blew up in mid-air and it too went down. I continued to fire at the remaining bombers, and when I ran out of ammunition only 4-5 SBs remained in the formation, including one trailing smoke.'

Nieminen (in FA-11) was credited with three kills and MSgt Por-

3/LeLv 24 leader Capt Jorma 'Joppe' Karhunen taxies out at the start of a combat sortie in BW-366 at Lappeenranta in August 1941. The 3rd flight used orange-coloured spinners and tail numbers, whilst the lynx emblem had originally been unique to Karhunen's flight, although it was soon adopted by the whole squadron

WO Veikko Rimminen taxies across a forest clearing towards the runway at Rantasalmi in 2/LeLv 24's BW-367 in July 1941. Delivered in a silver dope finish, the Brewsters were camouflaged when mobilisation was announced. Rimminen got his final kill on 8 September 1941, making him an ace. He flew 190 missions and finish-ed the war as an instructor (*A Donner*)

4/LeLv 24's BW-383 is seen after experiencing landing gear failure at Rantasalmi in July 1941. On top of his Winter War victories, Martti Alho scored a further 13.5 kills in this aircraft to raise his final tally to 15. Soon after becoming the youngest warrant officer in the air force, Alho was killed when wooden-winged BW-392 crashed on 5 June 1943

Five-victory ace 1Lt Veikko Evinen flew D.XXI FR-114 for a month in June/July 1941. On 25 June he destroyed two DB-3 bombers near Helsinki, although he was piloting FR-116 at the time. Later promoted to lead 3/HLeLv 32, Evinen was shot down and killed by ground fire exactly three years later whilst flying Curtiss Hawk CU-581

Mechanics can be seen winding the inertia starter of 2/LeLv 30 D.XXI FR-125 at Hyvinkää in this photograph, taken on 11 July 1941. Three days prior this shot being taken, 2Lt Ture Mattila had opened his score in this machine – he would remain its pilot until the end of the year. Note the different 'squiggle' patterns on the spats of the Fokker, this almost random style of camouflage being quite common amongst D.XXIs at the time (*SA-kuva*)

vari (in FA-20) 3.5 to make him an ace. Soviet records acknowledge the loss of nine SBs to '12 Bf 109s', of which they downed three!

The Soviet offensive on 25 June was focused exclusively on eastern Finland, with the units at Joroinen and Joensuu seeing virtually all the action. However, 1/LeLv 28 pilot Sgt Tani (in MS.406 MS311) and his wingman observed a lone, and obviously disoriented, SB (probably belonging to 10.SBAP) near their base and duly shot it down at 1300 hours.

A haul of 26 bombers destroyed (23 now acknowledged) was just the start the Finnish fighter force wanted to the Continuation War, although its ground-based early warning and fighter control system proved to be less than efficient – indeed, despite having 125 fighters on duty, less than a fifth engaged the enemy. This problem was slowly put right, however.

Soviet records claim that during the bomber offensive of 25 June-1 July, they attacked 39 Finnish (and German) airfields and destroyed 130

Having transferred to 1/LeLv 30 just three weeks previously, Ture Mattila proudly stands by the tail of FR-125 at Utti in mid-November 1941. The 'white 4' on the fighter's rudder was freshly applied upon its arrival at the new unit, replacing 2/LeLv 30's red and yellow tactical number. Mattila later flew Bf 109s with 1/LeLv 34, raising his tally to eight victories in 296 missions (*SA-kuva*)

aircraft on the ground. German records show no such losses, whilst the Finns had just two aircraft lightly damaged. On the other hand, Finnish fighters claimed 34 bombers destroyed during the same period.

On 4 July MSgt Tuominen scrambled in G.50 FA-3 to intercept 72.SBAP bombers sent to attack Joensuu. At 1000 m he engaged them;

'I observed the aircraft shortly after they had released their bombs, and they were surrounded by anti-aircraft fire. I came in just under the clouds, shooting out the left engine of the first bomber to enter my sights. I pressed home my attack to a distance of 50 m astern, and it caught fire.

4/LeLv 24 pilots are seen at Immola in late August 1941. They are, from left to right, Cpl Tapio Järvi, Sgt Aarne Korhonen, 2Lt Aulis Lumme, 1Lt Henrik Elfving, 1Lt Urho Sarjamo, Capt Per-Erik Sovelius, 1Lt Iikka Törrönen, SSgt Martti Alho and SSgt Jalo Dahl. All but Korhonen, Elfving and Dahl would achieve 'acedom' (*SA-kuva*)

'I fired at the second bomber from slightly side on, and it dropped away into a steepening dive trailing heavy smoke. Then I fired at three more aircraft, two of which also burst into flames. At this point my aircraft was hit in the fuel tank, and I quickly shot the gunner who had fired at me, resulting in his machine diving into cloud trailing smoke.

'The remaining bomber gunners then all seemed to fire at me at once, and due to my close range (between 30 and 100 m), my fighter was hit in

BW-378 was the mount of 4/LeLv 24's CO, Capt 'Pelle' Sovelius, until 16 February 1942, when he was posted to HQ – he later became a test pilot. Sovelius claimed seven victories in this fighter to raise his tally to 13 in 257 missions. BW-378 is seen at Vesivehmaa in May 1942 (*O Riekki*)

BW-376's 'team' pose for the camera at 1/LeLv 24's Rantasalmi airfield in July 1941. They are, from left to right, mechanic Sgt E Horppu, pilot WO V Pyötsiä and assistant mechanic J Salminen. 'Isä Vikki' ('Father Vikki') Pyötsiä was one of the air force's 'old hands', having been born in 1909. Despite his advancing years, he saw service with LeLv 24 throughout the various wars with the USSR (*V Lakio*)

the fuel tank (again) and in the rudder. Only one of my guns had been working all this time, as the ammunition belt of the other weapon had snapped off after my first burst.'

Tuominen claimed three SBs but was later credited with four after the wrecks of all of them were found – quite an achievement with just one synchronised 12.7 mm Breda gun.

## OFFENSIVE TO
## KARELIA

Following the successes of *Barbarossa*, the Finns hastily drew up an offensive plan of their own in late June 1941. It consisted of a two-phase assault on Karelia and a single attack across the Karelian Isthmus, the army's objective being to seize only those areas handed over to the USSR as part of the 1940 peace treaty.

For operations north of Lake Ladoga, a Karelian Army was formed, and it was assigned *Lentorykmentti* 2, with all three fighter squadrons plus LeLv 12 and LeLv 16 for reconnaissance and army co-operation duties. LeR 4 Blenheim bombers could also be called upon when needed.

The massing of Finnish troops in preparation for the offensive failed to escape detection by Soviet reconnaissance flights, and on 8 July air attacks commenced. Defending the assembled force, Brewster pilots shot down

Pyötsiä's mount is seen at Rantasalmi in July 1941. He scored 4.5 victories with this machine, raising his total in Brewsters to 8.5. During the summer of 1944 he engaged the Red Air Force flying a Bf 109G, achieving an additional 4.5 victories. Flying a total of 437 missions, Pyötsiä scored 19.5 aerial kills

1/LeLv 24 Brewster BW-390 taxies out at Nurmoila in October 1941. Whilst with this flight the aircraft was initially assigned to 2Lt Kai Matsola, who went on to score 6.5 victories in Brewsters and four in Bf 109Gs. His final tally of 10.5 kills was achieved during 296 missions (*V Lakio*)

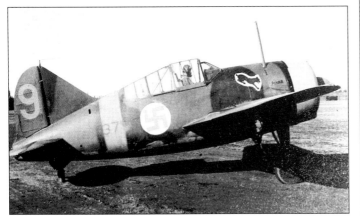

3/LeLv 24's deputy leader, 1Lt Pekka Kokko, was one of the top scoring Finnish aces of 1941, raising his tally to 13.5 victories. He used this Brewster (BW-379) for much of the year, as signified by the inscription of his christian name in small black letters immediately behind the engine cowling. Kokko became a test pilot on 24 November 1941, and was eventually killed in a flying accident on 19 February 1944

two bombers and six fighters in three engagements. Twenty-four hours later they were even more successful – 12 Brewsters from 3 and 4/LeLv 24 took off at 0400 on a combat air patrol led by Maj Magnusson, and 70 minutes later nine of them engaged 15 I-153s over Lahdenpohja. WO Juutilainen (in BW-364) participated in the combat;

'I noticed 1Lt Kokko and his wingman hit an I-153 formation. I also attacked this gaggle, followed by Cpl Huotari. I fired at close range and hit several planes. During my return to Lahdenpohja, I observed an I-153 at low altitude, so I dived after it and shot at it from a distance of 50 m and a height of just 10 m above the forest between Miinala and Lahdenpohja.

BW-368 of 3/LeLv 24 was photographed in a worn white distemper at Kontupohja in March 1942. The fighter was regularly flown by Sgt Nils Katajainen, and the fin shows his tally of six aircraft. Note also the 'yellow 1' painted on the green rudder. 'Nipa' Katajainen would eventually score 17.5 victories in Brewsters (*E Lyly*)

For the first year of the Continuation War Sgt Jouko 'Jussi' Huotari flew BW-353 with 3/LeLv 24, scoring eight kills. The aircraft is seen here at Lunkula (which was a very basic shore landing strip on the banks of Lake Ladoga) in September 1941. Huotari added a further eight kills in in Bf 109s in 1944 to raise his tally to 17.5 from 291 missions (*J Timonen*)

WO Oiva 'Oippa' Tuominen sits on the tail of his Fiat G.50 (FA-26) at Lunkula in August 1941. Shortly after this shot was taken he became the first knight of the Mannerheim Cross on 18 August due to his score of eight Winter War victories and 11.5 kills in the Continuation War. His elaborate scoreboard shows white kill bars for bomber victories, black/white for fighters and blue/white for flying boats. The horizontal bar denotes WO Lautamäki's kill in this aircraft on 13 August 1941
(*Finnish Aviation Museum*)

LeLv 26's Fiat *Schwarm* is seen at the Lunkula shore strip on 4 September 1941 after returning from a mission. The aircraft are, from left to right, FA-3, -35, -27 and -6, and pilots from all three of LeLv 26's flights are present according to the markings painted on the G.50s. FA-6 was regularly flown by 12.5 victory ace MSgt Onni Paronen (*SA-kuva*)

'Climbing back up, I spotted two I-153s that had escaped the initial interception heading towards Sorola island, so I followed them. I waited until the lead aircraft stopped taking evasive action and started flying straight and level before I dived in behind it and shot off five-six rounds with both fuselage guns (the wing guns did not work during the combat). The I-153 banked left and plunged belly up into Lake Ladoga. My engine then started to run roughly so I gave up chasing the third fighter.'

In ten minutes the Russians had lost eight I-153s destroyed and another four damaged, these being credited to six pilots – MSgt Nissinen (in BW-353) was the other double scorer. Flying an aircraft that was faster than most of its rivals, Brewster pilots had begun to employ 'pendulum' tactics, which they would use successfully for the next two years.

On 10 July the Karelian army commenced its offensive, and within six days it had seized the northern tip of Lake Ladoga. Two weeks later the army achieved its intermediary goal when it reached the River Tuulos, at which point C-in-C, Marshall Mannerheim, called a halt to the advance.

1/LeLv 32 leader Capt Paavo 'Pate' Berg uses a handy stick to point out patched bullet holes in Curtiss Hawk CUw-553 to his mechanic at Lappeenranta on 24 September 1941. The aircraft's original construction number 13663 is still partially visible on the fin in this photo. Having already 'made ace' during the Winter War, Berg had increased his score to 9.5 by the time he was shot down and killed in CUw-570 over Hanko on 1 November 1941 (*SA-kuva*)

LeLv 32 Hawk CUw-560 was photographed at Suulajärvi in April 1942. Unlike other units, LeLv 32 did not assign its aircraft to any particular pilot, although 20-year-old 2Lt 'Kössi' Karhila did become an ace in it on 19 September 1941, eventually scoring eight kills with the fighter. His total haul on Curtiss Hawks was 13, and he continued his run of success once issued with a Bf 109G in May 1943 (*P Saari*)

The offensive to capture the Karelian Isthmus started on 31 July, and LeLv 32, equipped with Hurricanes and Hawks (and fortified by 3/LeLv 24's Brewsters), provided aerial protection. The army pushed east of Viipuri and arrived on the banks of Lake Ladoga a week later. It eventually met up with the victorious Karelian army on 15 August. Viipuri was left in a siege until taken on 30 August. In just four days of fighting Finnish troops had chased the numerically superior Red Army to the old border, where it was told to stop. Leningrad was just 30 km further east.

On 12 August Capt Karhunen's six Brewsters had engaged some 20 I-153s hell bent on strafing troops on the Karelian Isthmus, the combat commencing at 1300 hours and finishing some 30 minutes later. Nine 'Chaikas' were destroyed, and all six Finnish pilots were credited with

1/LeLv 28 MS.406 MS-619 is seen parked on the grass at a sunny Solomanni, near Petrozavodsk, in the summer of 1942. This aircraft was assigned to SSgt Antti Tani on 4 October 1941, and he subsequently flew it for some 18 months. A solitary victory bar appeared on the fighter's fin on 25 March 1942 (a Pe-2), this being one of seven kills Tani scored in Moranes – only two (both Pe-2s) where claimed in this machine, however

MS-317 was also a 1/LeLv 28 machine, and it too is seen at Solomanni during the summer of 1942. During this time it was regularly flown by 2Lt Paavo 'Pampsa' Myllylä, who scored 1.5 victories in Moranes (both in this aircraft) and 19.5 kills in Bf 109Gs during 420 missions. The victory bars on this fighter indicate the score of the plane, rather than an individual – a common feature of LeLv 28's MS.406s

3/LeLv 28 MS.406s MS-315 and -329 at Solomanni in October 1941. The latter fighter with a yellow 1 on its tail was flown by 6.5-victory ace Sgt Toivo Tomminen. On 4 December 1941 he collided with a Hurricane of 152.IAP, flown by SrLt N F Repnikov, whilst flying this very aircraft – both pilots were killed

MS-318 of 2/LeLv 28 was photographed at Viitana in November 1941, this aircraft having been assigned to 2Lt Martti Inehmo the previous September. He remained its pilot until he went missing in action on 26 December 1941 whilst flying MS-618. Inehmo flew 87 missions and scored eight kills, including 'triples' on 9 September and 9 October 1941 (J Puolakkainen)

# MANNERHEIM CROSS

Following the end of the Winter War, the statute governing the creation of the Mannerheim Cross was issued on 16 December 1940. The recipient became a knight of the Mannerheim Cross, and it was awarded in two classes for extraordinary bravery, highly notable achievements in battle, or exceptionally outstanding leadership. Its awarding was not dependent on the rank of the nominee.

The first cross (No 1) was issued on 22 July 1941 to Col Ernst Lagus for heading armoured units in battle. The first air force Mannerheim Cross knight (No 6) was WO Oiva Tuominen, who received his award on 18 August 1941 for scoring 20 kills, eight of them in the Winter War – future winners had only their present achievements taken into account.

The Mannerheim Cross can be compared with the British Victoria Cross or the American Medal of Honor, being the highest military honour awarded in Finland. Some 191 were issued, with only four men receiving it twice – fighter pilots Capt Hans Wind and WO Ilmari Juutilainen on 28 June 1944, and Maj Gen Aaro Pajari and Col Martti Aho on 16 October 1944.

The Mannerheim Cross 1st class was issued only twice, to Marshal of Finland Carl Gustaf Emil Mannerheim himself on 17 October 1941 (No 18), and chief of the staff Gen Axel Heinrichs on 31 December 1944. The latter individual had earlier received the 2nd class award (No 48) on 5 February 1942. The sum of 5000 Finnmarks (then equal to the annual salary of a regular first lieutenant) was also presented to the recipient of the Mannerheim Cross.

kills, Juutilainen claiming a triple score and Katajainen a double.

The following day LeLv 26 escorted an artillery fire-control aircraft across Lake Ladoga to a position south of the River Tuulos. At 1400 hours, just as 1Lt Hämäläinen's *Schwarm* was being relieved by 1Lt Puhakka's flight, nine 'Chaikas' from 195 and 197.IAP attacked the observation aircraft. During the five minutes of combat which ensued, eight G.50s downed all the I-153s, with two falling to Puhakka in FA-1.

## — OCCUPATION OF OLONETS AND KARELIA —

On 3 September the Karelian army commenced its four-day advance on the River Svir. Having captured this objective, it continued to thrust both eastward and northward towards Petrozavodsk. The opening day of the offensive saw a *Schwarm* of G.50s from LeLv 26 patrolling over the spearhead and engaging three 'Chaikas' of 65.ShAP (assault aviation regiment) and two 'Ratas' of 155.IAP, all of which were shot down.

Following the halt of the Finnish advance on the Karelian Isthmus on

Leading Morane ace with 15 kills was MSgt Urho Lehtovaara, who is seen here taxying out in MS-327 at Viitana in December 1941. On the 23rd of that month this aircraft suffered a fire whilst being started, so Lehtovaara was issued with MS-304 instead. Later flying Bf 109Gs with 3/LeLv 34 from 28 March 1943, he scored 44.5 kills during 400+ missions. Lehtovaara received the Mannerheim Cross on 9 July 1944

2/LeLv 30 leader Capt Veikko Karu at the official ceremony to mark the awarding of his Mannerheim Cross on 6 November 1942. Having scored his kills in 1940-42, he then spent time in staff postings until 6 March 1944, when was given command of HLeLv 30 (*SA-kuva*)

Wasp-powered D.XXI FR-129 was photographed at Suulajärvi in November 1941. Issued with this aircraft at the start of the Continuation War, Capt Karu subsequently flew FR-129 for 17 months, claiming half of his ten kills in it. His flight also sank 17 light surface vessels in the Gulf of Finland (*A Bremer*)

3 September, LeLv 32's Capt Berg led seven Hawks across the Soviet border for a 15-minute battle with I-153s of 5.AD (aviation division) – each of the Finnish pilots involved claimed single kills.

Six days later a 2/LeLv 28 *Schwarm* engaged nine 'Chaikas' and six 'Ratas' of 155.IAP over the River Svir, shooting six of them down. On the return flight to base, the MS.406s bounced three bombers, escorted by five fighters, and the Soviets duly lost two more I-153s – both 2Lt Inehmo (in MS-623) and SSgt Lehtovaara (in MS-304) claimed three kills apiece.

As the advancing Karelian army closed on Petrozavodsk, LeLv 24 continued to fly top cover. On 23 September, Capt Karhunen led eight Brewsters against three I-16s from 155.IAP caught strafing troops. Enjoying odds firmly stacked in their favour for a change, the Finnish pilots quickly destroyed the 'Ratas'. Following a pre-briefed plan, Karhunen then ordered his flight (by radio) to return to base, whilst he circled for half an hour at low level over the wilderness in complete radio silence. He then flew back to the troop emplacements, where he bounced six more 155.IAP I-16s strafing the infantry. Only one escaped.

Three days later Karhunen repeated the same tactic, with his flight destroying all six 'Chaikas' initially encountered. Circling at tree-top height for a short while, the Brewsters returned to find three I-16s, three I-15bis and two I-153s of 65.ShAP harassing the troops. Three Russians were promptly downed, whilst the others fled the area. Juutilainen scored three in BW-364 and Karhunen two in BW-366.

Following the capture of Olonets and Petrozavodsk by 1 October, the

Karelian army advanced slowly northward along the west coast of Lake Onega. Once at the northern tip of the lake, the Finns occupied the towns of Karhumäki and Poventsa on 5/6 December, thus ending their advance. From these defensive positions, a two-and-a-half-year stationary war now began.

During 1941 LeLv 24 had claimed 135 victories without losing a single Brewster to fighters. LeLv 26 had downed 52 aircraft with its Fiats, also without any combat losses. LeLv 28 scored 70 kills for the loss of five Moranes in combat, whilst LeLv 32 had destroyed 52 aircraft with its Curtiss Hawks, but had also lost five of its number to enemy fighters.

The ace list for the Continuation War was as follows at the end of 1941;

3/LeLv 30 (ex-1/LeLv 10) D.XXI FR-148 was photographed at Tiiksjärvi on 4 November 1941, having just exchanged its wheels for skis. Flown by the unit's top scorer, 1Lt Martti Kalima, during the first 12 months of the war, FR-148 was used by him to claim three victories (*SA-kuva*)

| Rank | Name | Squadron | Victories |
|------|------|----------|-----------|
| WO | Tuominen, Oiva | 26 | 13 |
| WO | Juutilainen, Ilmari | 24 | 13 |
| MSgt | Nissinen, Lauri | 24 | 13 |
| 1Lt | Kokko, Pekka | 24 | 10 |
| MSgt | Lehtovaara, Urho | 28 | 10 |
| Capt | Karhunen, Jorma | 24 | 8.5 |
| 2Lt | Inehmo, Martti | 28 | 7 |
| MSgt | Kinnunen, Eero | 24 | 6.5 |
| Sgt | Tomminen, Toivo | 28 | 6.5 |
| Capt | Nieminen, Urho | 26 | 6 |
| 1Lt | Puhakka, Olli | 26 | 6 |
| Sgt | Katajainen, Nils | 24 | 6 |
| Capt | Luukkanen, Eino | 24 | 5.5 |
| Capt | Sovelius, Per-Erik | 24 | 5 |
| 2Lt | Karhila, Kyösti | 32 | 5 |
| SSgt | Tani, Antti | 28 | 5 |
| Sgt | Kirjonen, Mauno | 32 | 5 |

This 4 November 1941 close-up of the tail of FR-148 shows 'Masa' Kalima's four confirmed aerial victories (his fourth was scored in FR-150 on 27 September 1941), plus one damaged. On 1 August 1942 Kalima's 3/LeLv 30 was merged with LeLv 14, and he subsequently joined the MS.406-equipped 1st flight (*SA-kuva*)

# COLOUR PLATES

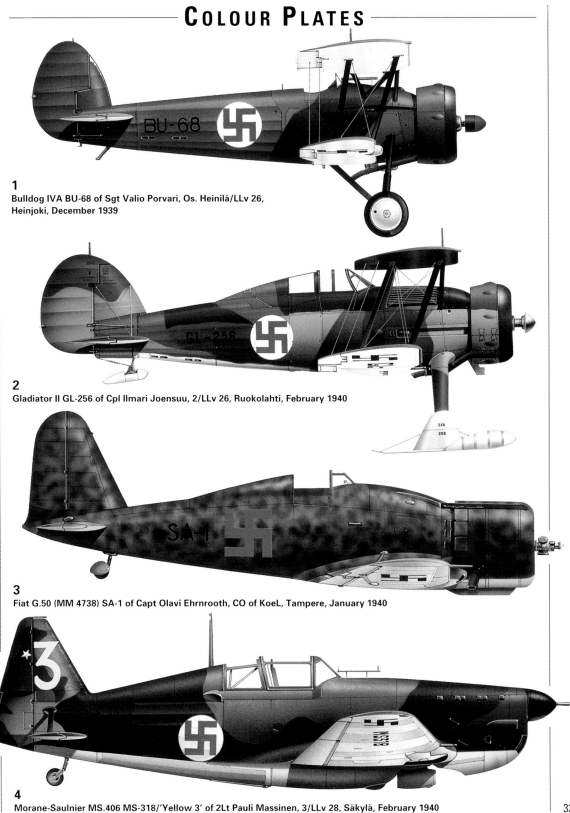

**1**
Bulldog IVA BU-68 of Sgt Valio Porvari, Os. Heinilä/LLv 26,
Heinjoki, December 1939

**2**
Gladiator II GL-256 of Cpl Ilmari Joensuu, 2/LLv 26, Ruokolahti, February 1940

**3**
Fiat G.50 (MM 4738) SA-1 of Capt Olavi Ehrnrooth, CO of KoeL, Tampere, January 1940

**4**
Morane-Saulnier MS.406 MS-318/'Yellow 3' of 2Lt Pauli Massinen, 3/LLv 28, Säkylä, February 1940

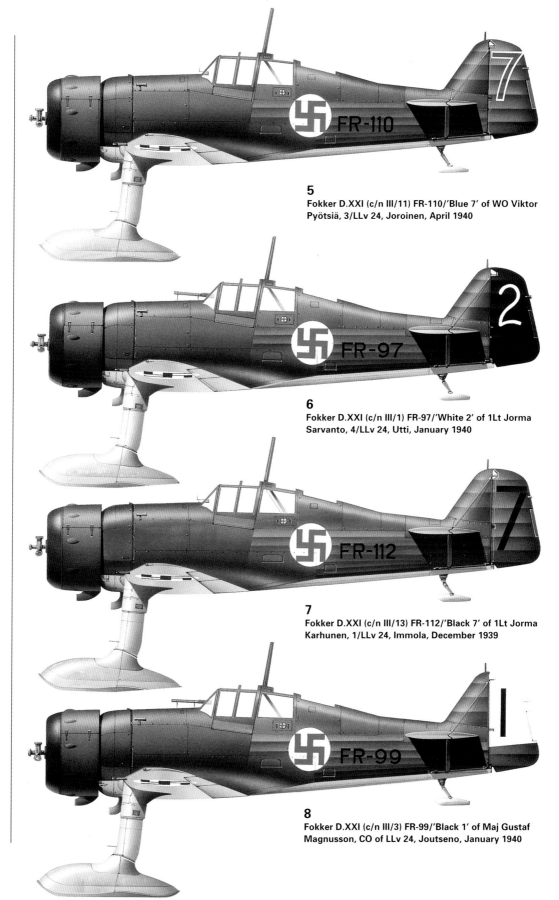

**5**
Fokker D.XXI (c/n III/11) FR-110/'Blue 7' of WO Viktor
Pyötsiä, 3/LLv 24, Joroinen, April 1940

**6**
Fokker D.XXI (c/n III/1) FR-97/'White 2' of 1Lt Jorma
Sarvanto, 4/LLv 24, Utti, January 1940

**7**
Fokker D.XXI (c/n III/13) FR-112/'Black 7' of 1Lt Jorma
Karhunen, 1/LLv 24, Immola, December 1939

**8**
Fokker D.XXI (c/n III/3) FR-99/'Black 1' of Maj Gustaf
Magnusson, CO of LLv 24, Joutseno, January 1940

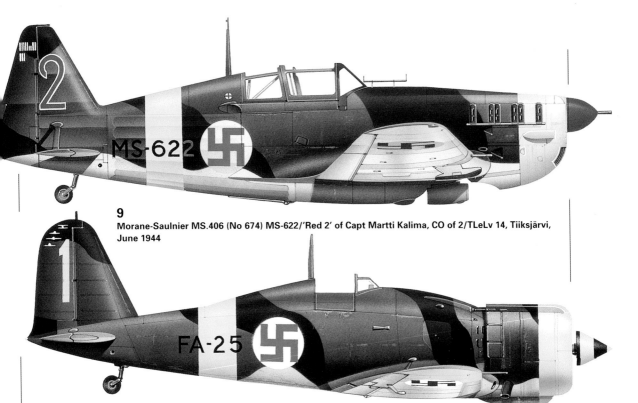

**9**
Morane-Saulnier MS.406 (No 674) MS-622/'Red 2' of Capt Martti Kalima, CO of 2/TLeLv 14, Tiiksjärvi, June 1944

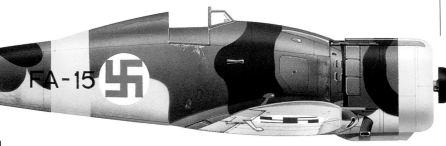

**10**
Fiat G.50 (MM 3614) FA-25/'Yellow 1' of Capt Olli Puhakka, CO of 3/LeLv 26, Kilpasilta, December 1942

**11**
Fiat G.50 (MM 4736) FA-15/'Yellow 5' of Sgt Klaus Alakoski, 3/LeLv 26, Kilpasilta, November 1942

**12**
Polikarpov I-153 IT-18/'Grey 8' of 2Lt Olavi Puro, 3/LeLv 6, Römpötti, November 1942

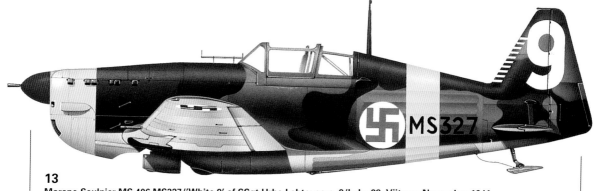

**13**
Morane-Saulnier MS.406 MS327/'White 9' of SSgt Urho Lehtovaara, 2/LeLv 28, Viitana, November 1941

**14**
Morane-Saulnier MS.406 MS-317/'Black 2' of 1Lt Paavo Myllylä, 1/LeLv 28, Äänislinna, July 1942

**15**
Fiat G.50 (MM 4743) FA-26/'White 5' of WO Oiva Tuominen, 1/LeLv 26, Kilpasilta, October 1942

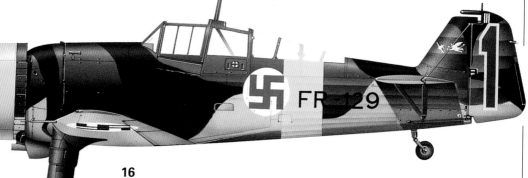

**16**
Fokker D.XXI (c/n IV/12) FR-129/'Red 1' of Capt Veikko Karu, CO of 2/LeLv 30, Suulajärvi, November 1941

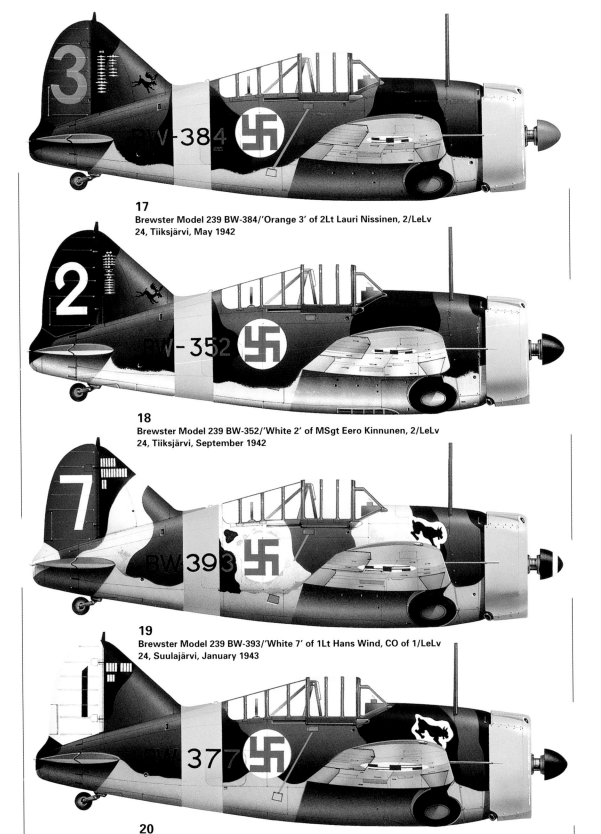

**17**
Brewster Model 239 BW-384/'Orange 3' of 2Lt Lauri Nissinen, 2/LeLv 24, Tiiksjärvi, May 1942

**18**
Brewster Model 239 BW-352/'White 2' of MSgt Eero Kinnunen, 2/LeLv 24, Tiiksjärvi, September 1942

**19**
Brewster Model 239 BW-393/'White 7' of 1Lt Hans Wind, CO of 1/LeLv 24, Suulajärvi, January 1943

**20**
Brewster Model 239 BW-377/'Black 1' of SSgt Tapio Järvi, 4/LeLv 24, Römpötti, October 1942

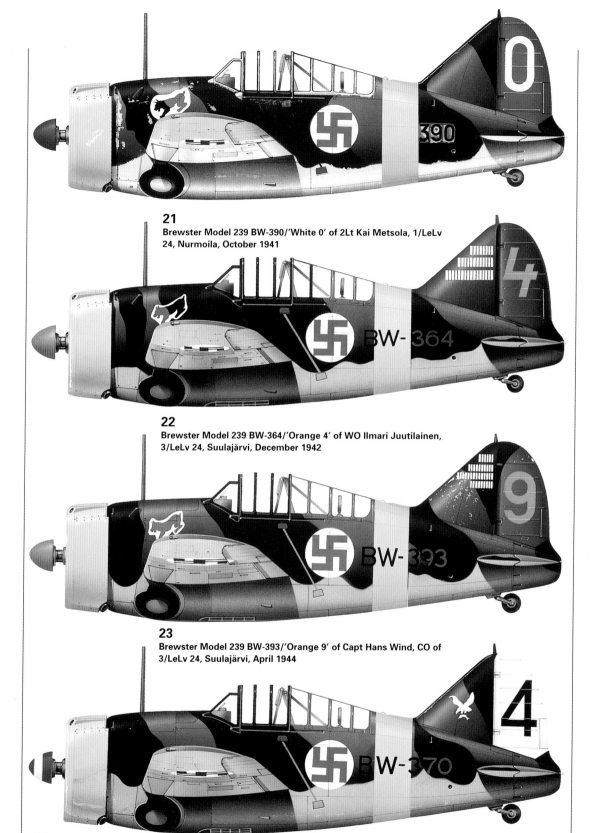

**21**
Brewster Model 239 BW-390/'White 0' of 2Lt Kai Metsola, 1/LeLv 24, Nurmoila, October 1941

**22**
Brewster Model 239 BW-364/'Orange 4' of WO Ilmari Juutilainen, 3/LeLv 24, Suulajärvi, December 1942

**23**
Brewster Model 239 BW-393/'Orange 9' of Capt Hans Wind, CO of 3/LeLv 24, Suulajärvi, April 1944

**24**
Brewster Model 239 BW-370/'Black 4' of 1Lt Aulis Lumme, 4/LeLv 24, Römpötti, October 1942

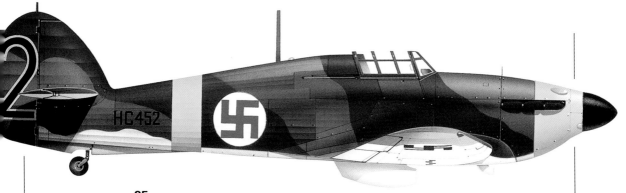

**25**
Hurricane I (N2394) HC452/'Black 2' of SSgt Lauri Jutila, LeLv 32, Suulajärvi, May 1942

**26**
Curtiss Hawk 75A-6 (c/n 13644) CUw-560/'Yellow 0' of 2Lt Kyösti Karhila, 1/LeLv 32, Lappeenranta, September 1941

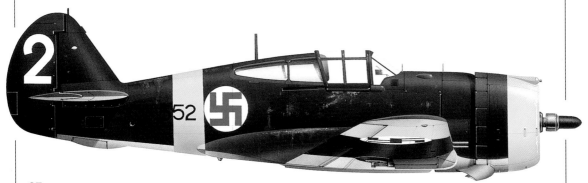

**27**
Curtiss Hawk 75A-3 (c/n 13747) CU-552/'White 2' of 2Lt Kalevi Tervo, 2/LeLv 32, Nurmoila, June 1942

**28**
Curtiss Hawk 75A-2 (No 170) CU-581/'Blue 1' of Capt Veikko Evinen, CO of 3/HLeLv 32, Nurmoila, March 1944

**29**
Bf 109G-2 (Wk-Nr 14718) MT-201/'White 1' of Maj Eino Luukkanen, CO of LeLv 34, Utti, June 1943

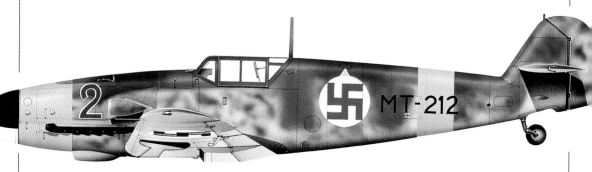

**30**
Bf 109G-2 (Wk-Nr 14753) MT-212/'Red 2' of WO Ilmari Juutilainen, 1/LeLv 34, Utti, May 1943

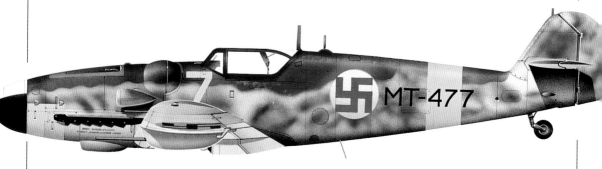

**31**
Bf 109G-6/R6 (Wk-Nr 165249) MT-477/'Yellow 7' of 1Lt Mikko Pasila, 1/HLeLv 24, Lappeenranta, July 1944

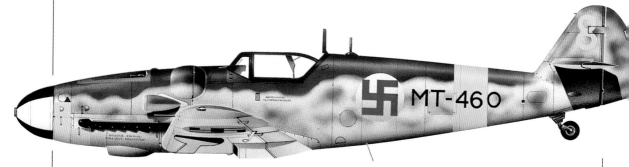

**32**
Bf 109G-6 (Wk-Nr 165001) MT-460/'Yellow 8' of SSgt Emil Vesa, 3/HLeLv 24, Lappeenranta, July 1944

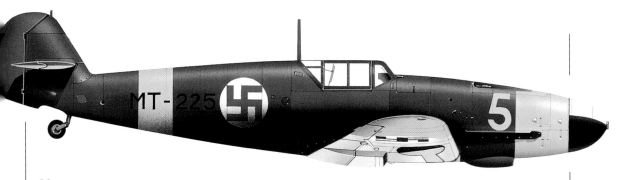

**33**
Bf 109G-2 (Wk-Nr 13577) MT-225/'Yellow 5' of 1Lt Lauri Nissinen, CO of 1/HLeLv 24, Suulajärvi, May 1944

**34**
Bf 109G-6 (Wk-Nr 412122) MT-423/'White 3' of SSgt Hemmo Leino, 1/HLeLv 34, Kymi, June 1944

**35**
Bf 109G-6/R6 (Wk-Nr 165342) MT-461/'Yellow 6' of 1Lt Kyösti Karhila, CO of 3/HLeLv 24, Lappeenranta, July 1944

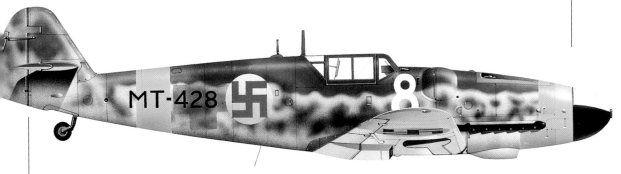

**36**
Bf 109G-6 (Wk-Nr 411901) MT-428/'White 8' of MSgt Antti Tani, 1/HLeLv 34, Lappeenranta, June 1944

**37**
Bf 109G-2 (Wk-Nr 14754) MT-213/'White 3' of 1Lt Eero Riihikallio, 2/HLeLv 24, Suulajärvi, May 1944

**38**
Bf 109G-6 (Wk-Nr 166007) MT-487/'Yellow 7' of WO Mauno Fräntilä, 2/HLeLv 30, Kymi, August 1944

**39**
Bf 109G-6 (Wk-Nr 164943) MT-433/'Yellow 3' of Capt Olli Puhakka, CO of 3/HLeLv 34, Taipalsaari, August 1944

**40**
Bf 109G-6 (Wk-Nr 165461) MT-476/'Yellow 7' of MSgt Nils Katajainen, 3/HLeLv 24, Lappeenranta, July 1944

**1**
SSgt Nils Katajainen of 3/LeLv 24 at
Suulajärvi in May 1943

**2**
WO Viktor Pyötsiä of 3/LLv 24 at
Värtsilä in January 1940

**3**
Capt Aulis Bremer, CO of 2/LeLv 32 at
Suulajärvi in April 1942

**4**
1Lt Hans Wind, CO of 3/LeLv 24 at
Suulajärvi in August 1943

**5**
1Lt Kyösti Karhila, CO of 3/HLeLv 24
at Lappeenranta in July 1944

**6**
WO Ilmari Juutilainen of 1/HLeLv 34
at Taipalsaari in July 1944

# FIGHTING LEND-LEASE

In August 1941 Lend-Lease shipments of Hurricanes started to arrive in significant at the Soviet arctic ports of Murmansk and Arkhangelsk arctic from the UK. Once reassembled, these fighters were primarily deployed against the Germans by the Northern Fleet air forces in the Murmansk and Kandalaksha areas. However, as more aircraft arrived in the USSR, regular air force units along the Finnish border also started to re-equip with Hurricane IIAs and IIBs.

The first Finnish identification of a Hurricane was made on 17 December 1941 when Capt Karhunen's *Schwarm* engaged nine fighters west of the White Sea near Belomorsk. In the ensuing clash, one Hurricane of 152.IAP and four I-153s of 65.ShAP were claimed to have been shot down.

Recent research has shown that 11 days prior to this 'first' encounter with Soviet Hurricanes, 6.5 kill ace Sgt Toivo Tomminen of 3/LeLv 28 had actually collided with a 152.IAP Hawker fighter, flown by SrLt N F Repnikov, over Karhumäki. Both the MS.406 (MS-329) and the Hurricane were destroyed in the collision, which also killed the pilots. The British fighter had been misidentified as a MiG-3 at the time.

As Hurricanes started to reach units south of Murmansk, LeLv 14, at the northern most Finnish airfield of Tiiksjärvi (200 km west of Belomorsk, on the White Sea), found that they could not repel the increasing numbers of Soviet Hawker fighters appearing in their sector with their ageing D.XXIs.

Accordingly, on 8 January 1942 the eight Brewsters of 2/LeLv 24 were posted 'temporarily' to Tiiksjärvi, and within two weeks the flight had been further strengthened with the addition of four more aircraft. Just 24 hours after their arrival, the airfield was strafed by six Hurricanes, which were in turn intercepted by four D.XXIs that managed to get airborne during the attack. A solitary kill was achieved by the Finnish pilots, future ace Sgt Hemmo Leino, flying FR-146, claiming his first victory (of an eventual tally of 11).

On 24 January 2/LeLv 24 engaged the enemy for the first time in the Rukajärvi area when five Brewsters ran into ten I-15bis and I-153 fighters from 65.ShAP and claimed four of them shot down. A fifth Soviet fighter was also destroyed when SrLt V A Knizhnik deliberately rammed (dubbed a 'taran' attack – see *Aircraft of the Aces 15 - Soviet Aces of World*

2/LeLv 24's deputy leader, 1Lt Lauri Pekuri, poses with his pipe between sorties in August 1942. During the previous spring and summer he had led the Brewsters of this flight in a series of successful actions against Lend-Lease Hurricanes, claiming seven destroyed himself. On 9 February 1943 he was transferred to 1/LeLv 34, which he led until 16 June 1944 when he was shot down in Bf 109G-6 MT-420 and made a PoW. Pekuri had scored 18.5 victories in 314 missions prior to being captured (*SA-kuva*)

*War 2* for further details) his I-153 into Sgt P Koskela's BW-372, the 'Chaika' making a forced landing and the Brewster returning to base. Both pilots claimed an aerial victory.

During February the Brewsters engaged Hurricanes on two occasions, claiming three destroyed both times, but March proved to be quiet. However, this was very much the 'lull before storm', as the communists had decided to destroy the Tiiksjärvi base once and for all.

## SUURSAARI OPERATION

The island of Suursaari is located south of Kotka in the middle of the Gulf of Finland. It was held by the Russians until early December 1941, when they evacuated their base in the face of Finnish advances. However, a realisation of its strategic importance soon after saw Red Army forces re-occupy the island on 2 January 1942. This latter action in turn prompted the Finnish army to take the island back whilst its troops could still safely advance over the ice.

Accordingly, on 27 March a 3500-man occupation force started the advance on Suursaari, supported by air cover to the tune of 57 aircraft – five captured SB bombers and six I-153 fighters from LeLv 6, six Brewsters from LeLv 24, sixteen D.XXIs from LeLv 30, thirteen Curtiss Hawks from LeLv 32 and eleven Blenheims from LeLv 42.

The 27th saw Finnish pilots shoot down four defending fighters, and 24 hours later two large-scale engagements took place. At 0800 1Lt Kauppinen led his *Schwarm* of Brewsters against ten I-153s of 71.IAP claiming exactly half their number shot down. Later that same day the island was taken by Finnish troops, and at 1740 12 Hawks led by 1Lt Nurminen intercepted 29 Soviet aircraft of 11.IAP and 71.IAP approaching in three groups. Whilst an impromptu victory parade continued on the ground, the Curtiss pilots scythed into their Soviet counterparts during a 20-minute melee which saw ten I-153s and five I-16s reportedly shot down without any losses to the Hawk flight. Soviet loss records for this action

2/LeLv 24 Brewster BW-372 is seen moments before commencing its take-off run at Tiiksjärvi on 25 May 1942. This aircraft was flown by 'Lasse' Pekuri until 25 June 1942, when he was shot down in it. He did, however, manage to escape through enemy territory until reaching the Finnish frontline (*SA-kuva*)

**Right**
2/LeLv 24 pilot 1Lt Lauri Nissinen is also seen in the throes of preparing for take-off in BW-384 at Tiiksjärvi on 25 May 1942. His fighter appears to still be wearing 3rd flight colours, judging by the darker number 3 on its rudder. Nissinen flew this aircraft for almost a year until 1 July 1942, when he was posted to the cadet school. Five days later he was awarded the Mannerheim Cross, having scored 25 aerial victories – of which exactly half were achieved whilst at the controls of this fighter (*SA-kuva*)

2/LeLv 24 fighters patrol the skies over Tiiksjärvi in September 1942. BW-352 was flown by WO Eero Kinnunen until he was shot down and killed by flak in it on 21 April 1943. The fin carries his victory marks and the flight emblem. 'Lekkeri' ('Flagon') Kinnunen flew over 300 missions and claimed 22.5 kills – 15 in this aircraft alone (*P Ervi*)

acknowledge the destruction of one I-15bis, one I-16 and six I-153s.

## EASTER AT TIIKSJÄRVI

On 29 March seven Hurricanes strafed the Tiiksjärvi base, and in response 1Lt Pekuri (in BW-372) led eight Brewsters on a reconnaissance mission to Segesha 24 hours later. Some 12 Hurricanes of 152.IAP were duly bounced during the offensive sweep and six were shot down.

Eight days later the Soviets carried out their long-planned air raid on

Part of the same formation as seen on the previous page, SSgt Heimo Lampi flies BW-354 over Tiiksjärvi in September 1942. As a member of 2/LeLv 24, he flew this particular Brewster for a period of 18 months in 1941/42, scoring his first 4.5 kills with it. Lampi was eventually commissioned to the rank of second lieutenant and went on to fly Bf 109Gs with 1/HLeLv 24, raising his score to 13.5 in 268 missions (*P Ervi*)

Aces of 3/LeLv 24 are seen at Hirvas on 27 June 1942. From left to right, they are SSgt 'Jussi' Huotari (17.5 kills), WO 'Illu' Juutilainen (94 kills), who is sitting on the tailplane of his BW-364, and Sgt 'Emppu' Vesa (29.5 victories). Vesa had scored his first kill (a Hurricane) just two days prior to this photograph being taken (*SA-kuva*)

Tiiksjärvi, this operation being undertaken in order to destroy the Finnish fighter force operating from the airfield either on the ground or in the air. Thirty-five aircraft were assembled for the attack, comprising eight Pe-2s from 608.PBAP, seven SBs from 80.BAP, nine Hurricanes from 767.IAP and three LaGG-3s and a further eight Hurricanes from 609.IAP. The raid had originally been scheduled for 5 April, but bad weather forced the attackers to to turn back. The following they tried again, only to be recalled when most of the escorting fighters failed to locate the bombers, and it was discovered that formation members had been issued with differing radio codes.

Finally, that afternoon a reduced force of seven bombers and eighteen fighters at last struck out for Tiiksjärvi. The presence of the Soviet formation was quickly detected through Finnish radio intelligence, however,

4/LeLv 24's BW-370 is seen at Römpötti in August 1942. It was regularly flown by 1Lt Aulis Lumme, who scored 4.5 of his total of 16.5 victories (in 287 missions) with the Brewster. 4/LeLv 24 used a stylised 'Osprey' as its flight emblem until 11 February 1943, when it reformed as the 2nd flight

3/LeLv 26 Fiat G.50 FA-1 sits with its engine protected from the cold at a snowy Helsinki Malmi in March 1942 – each fighter flight undertook one month shifts in defence of the capital. 1Lt Olli Puhakka flew this aircraft during the Finnish advance into the USSR in 1941, claiming six victories, as elaborately marked on the rudder of the Italian fighter (*C-E Bruun*)

and an interception vector was duly radioed to 1Lt Pekuri, who was leading 2/LeLv 24 on a routine patrol at the time. Intercepting the Soviet formation just minutes before its arrived over the Finnish airfield, the eight Brewster pilots succeeded in downing two DB-3 bombers (they were actually SBs from 80.BAP) and twelve Hurricanes without losses. During the action, which lasted 25 minutes (from 1525 to 1550 hours), 2Lt Lauri Nissinen (in BW-384) succeeded in downing three aircraft, as he explained in his report;

'I flew as a lead plane in the top *Schwarm*. We were returning from a recce from Belomorsk when we were alerted by radio of 25 Russian aircraft. We started to climb while heading towards the enemy. A big turning combat then started with the fighters. At first I fired at several planes, but was too busy to follow any.

49

3/LeLv 26 G.50 FA-33 has been parked in a wooden blast pen at Kilpasilta on 3 September 1942. MSgt Onni Paronen flew this fighter throughout the latter half of this year, claiming two victories (both I-16s). On 23 March 1943 Paronen was posted to LeLv 34 to fly Bf 109Gs, and he finished the war with 12.5 kills in 316 sorties (*SA-kuva*)

'After shooting at one Hurricane it went into a half roll and dived. I followed and fired a short burst at close range, sending the machine vertically into the forest trailing smoke. After the battle had gone on for ten minutes, the remaining Russians broke off and headed home. Over Ruka-järvi, I spotted an enemy aircraft at a height of 500 m, and I managed to close up on him until opening fire from obliquely behind at a distance of 50 m. Just after pulling the trigger it exploded. I did not have time to pull aside, and a piece of the Hurricane snapped off one of my exhaust pipes.

'I then joined 1Lt Pekuri and Sgt Korhonen in the chase of two remaining Hurricanes. When the one of them tried to bank towards Pekuri, I slipped in behind his tail, and then the Russian took evasive action. I managed to cause the Hurricane to smoke with my fire, and after a short chase it dived into the forest. In spite of numerical superiority, the Russians did nothing but attempt to evade our attacks. They appeared to be very helpless. No hits to my plane. Exhaust pipe shot off.'

Mentioned above in Nissinen's report, fellow ace 1Lt Lauri Pekuri also enjoyed success during the interception by downing a trio of Hurricanes (in BW-372);

'We met the enemy about 20 km from the airfield and I attacked the fighters, leaving two Brewsters to go after the bombers. I shot my first fighter down about five kilometres south-east of the base, where it burned on the ground. The second I hit in the engine and cooler, leaving the plane smoking heavily 800 m south of Ontrosenvaara – the wreck was later found here.

'Finally, in a chase just above the ground I shot my third Hurricane down into a ridge covered by forest half a kilometre west of the southern tip of Lake Rukajärvi. The pilot was captured in a wounded condition. The Hurricanes engaged all had 12 guns, and the pilots flying them appeared to be generally helpless.'

One pilot who actually achieved acedom as a result of his success on 6

Curtiss aces of LeLv 32 pose for a formal photo at Suulajärvi on 29 April 1942. They are, from left to right, WO Eino Koskinen (12.5 victories), 2nd flight leader Capt Aulis Bremer (8 victories), 1st flight leader Capt Kullervo Lahtela (10.5 victories), 3rd flight leader 1Lt Pentti Nurminen (6 victories) and Sgt Jaakko Kajanto (5 victories) (*SA-kuva*)

LeLv 32 Hawk CU-503 was photographed at Nurmoila, on the Olonets Isthmus, in July 1942. This fighter (c/n 13816) was originally a Cyclone-powered A-4, but it was re-engined with a license-built Twin Wasp once in Finland. Various LeLv 32 pilots claimed an accumulated total of ten victories while flying this aircraft (*A Bremer*)

Hawk 75A-6 CUw-558 of LeLv 32 is seen parked in the open at Nurmoila on 2 August 1942. Over a period of 18 months no fewer than 17 victories were scored with this aircraft, five of which fell to 11-victory ace SSgt Niilo Erkinheimo. The latter individual was to subsequently lose his life on 16 November 1943 when his Bf 109G (MT-223) caught fire in flight, forcing him to ditch in icy water. Erkinheimo drowned before he could be rescued (*Finnish Air Force*)

Successful LeLv 32 second lieutenants Yrjö Pallasvuo and Kalevi Tervo are seen in July 1942. 'Kreivi' ('Count') Pallasvuo scored nine victories in Hawks and a further four in Bf 109s, whilst 'Kale' Tervo finished with a tally of 23.25 kills. No fewer than 15.5 of these were scored in the Curtiss fighter, making him the type's top ace (*A Bremer*)

LeLv 32's CU-552 is parked in amongst the trees at Nurmoila in July 1942, 12.5 victory ace WO Eino Koskinen sat in its cockpit. This fighter achieved 15 kills, five of which fell Kalevi Tervo. The ace scored his final seven victories with 1/LeLv 34 in Bf 109Gs prior to being killed in action in MT-219 on 20 August 1943 (*A Bremer*)

April was 22-year-old Sgt Eino Peltola, whose double Hurricane haul, flying BW-379, repeated his score achieved again in this aircraft on the 30 March sweep to Segesha, which was detailed earlier in this chapter. His combat report was as follows;

'I was part of 1Lt Pekuri's flight, heading the second pair in his *Schwarm*. We got a message that seven bombers and 18 fighters were approaching, and we soon found them. After our first diving attack, I managed to set one of the Hurricanes alight, and it made a forced landing about 15 km south of Tiiksjärvi

'I caught the second Hurricane in the cockpit as it was banking. The plane went into a vertical dive and crashed into a swamp from a height of 500 m, catching fire and exploding on impact. The location of this crash site was north of Rikajärvi.'

Eino Peltola would eventually score 10.5 kills in 200+ sorties prior to his death on 2 April 1944, 7.5 of these being achieved in Brewsters and the remaining three in Bf 109Gs.

Whilst the Hurricane pilots had reportedly offered little resistance to the Brewsters, the bombers proved to be worthy opponents for the two

1Lt Jaakko Hillo flies LeLv 32's CU-580 over the River Svir on 16 October 1943. He served exclusively with this unit when in the frontline, scoring eight confirmed victories in 220 missions – including a half-share of a Il-2 in this very fighter on 22 June 1944 (*SA-kuva*)

pilots sent to shoot them down. Indeed, 1Lt Lasse Kilpinen (flying BW-394) suffered a serious calf injury when the tail gunner from the SB he was later credited with having destroyed managed to hit him with return fire on his second pass.

Official Soviet losses are known to have amounted to one SB from 80.BAP, two Hurricanes from 609.IAP and a further four from of 767.IAP. In return, the communists claimed four aircraft destroyed on the ground and seven Brewsters in the air. Following the poor results of this raid, the Red Air Force was not seen again until 8 June, when 1Lt Pekuri's six Brewsters engaged thirteen Hurricanes from the Kësa-based 152.IAP, sending five down but also losing one of their own.

On 25 June the last big combat took place north-east of Lake Seesjärvi when *Schwarms* from both 2 and 3/LeLv 24 engaged in a 15-fight fight with Hurricanes from 609.IAP. The Finns claimed four shot down and their Russian counterparts three, and on this occasion they were not far off the mark, as two Brewsters were lost, although both pilots survived.

In six months some 45 Hurricanes were claimed to have been shot down, which is not an unreasonable tally bearing in mind that during this period the average strength of an IAP numbered 15-20 serviceable fighters. Their job done, the Brewsters pilots would remain mostly unem-

1/LeLv 28 ace MSgt Antti Tani and his mechanic, Risto Hiltunen, pose alongside the tail of MS.406 MS-619 at Solomanni in March 1943. Tani's score then stood at seven in Moranes (two in this aircraft), and he later increased it to 21.5 flying Bf 109Gs with LeLv 34 from 15 April 1943 until war's end (*R Hiltunen*)

Prototype Mörkö (Ghost) Morane MS-631 is seen at Tampere in February 1943. Fitted with captured 1100 hp Klimov M-105 engines acquired from the Germans, some 41 MS.406s were so modified, boasting more streamlined cooling radiators. Finland's last – and youngest, at 21 – fighter ace, SSgt Lars Hattinen of 1/HLeLv 28, achieved three victories in Mörkö Moranes (the only kills scored by the fighter) on 16 (Yak-1) and 30 (two Airacobras) July 1944, the first of which was scored in this particular aircraft (*Finnish Aviation Museum*)

ployed at Tiiksjärvi until November 1942.

These final engagements in June signalled the start of a six-month period of relative stability along the Soviet frontlines, allowing the air force's senior staff to reorganise its fighter squadrons so as to offer Finland a better area defence system. However, air regiment commanders 'in the field' considered that the new strategy would result in their units losing an element of combat flexibility, which had been the main tactical advantage employed so effectively by Finnish fighter units up to this point in the war.

2/TLeLv 14 leader, and 10.5-kill ace (in 285 missions), Capt Martti Kalima is seen standing in front of his MS-622 at Tiiksjärvi in June 1944. On 14 June 1944 he led a group of pilots to Germany for nightfighter training, but returned following the signing of the truce with the USSR to become 2/HLeLv 30's leader on 14 September 1944 (*R Rosenberg*)

Nevertheless, on 3 May 1942 the front was divided into three sectors, with a single regiment then placed in charge of defending the airspace within that particular sector. The Lake Onega sector was covered by LeR 2, comprising LeLv 16, 24 and 28, Olonets belonged to LeR 1, with LeLv 12 and 32, and the Karelian Isthmus remained with LeR 3, controlling LeLv 26 and 30. The northern flank was covered with LeLv 14, whilst in the south LeLv 6 handled the Gulf of Finland. The bomber regiment LeR 4 was used wherever needed.

The system received further adjustment on 18 July 1942 when LeLv 24 was transferred to LeR 3, whilst on 16 November LeR 5 was formed to control LeLv 6 and 30 in the maritime patrol role. Finally, on 23 January 1943 LeLv 34 was also transferred to LeR 3.

'Masa' Kalima sits strapped into 1/LeLv 14 MS.406 MS-611 at Tiiksjärvi in March 1943. This aircraft was usually flown by fellow ace Sgt Aaro Nuorala until 9 April 1943, when he was transferred to LeLv 34 to fly Bf 109Gs. The latter pilot scored 14.5 kills, one of which (an I-15bis) was claimed in this aircraft on 16 March 1943. The flight's Moranes carried white tail numbers that went up to 18 (*K Temmes*)

# GULF OF FINLAND

When the ice melted in the Gulf of Finland in May 1942, the Red Banner Baltic Fleet started sending out submarines into the coastal shipping lanes from its huge naval (and air) base at Kronstadt, just outside Leningrad. These vessels had retreated into port the previous autumn, and with the spring thaw, their sole purpose now was to harass German and Finnish commercial shipping in the Baltic Sea The early summer saw the Red Banner Baltic Fleet air force increased in size so as to cover naval movements in the area – especially the submarine departures and arrivals in the eastern Gulf of Finland.

To counter the growing aerial activity LeLv 24 was seconded to LeR 3 on 18 July, and 3 and 4/LeLv 24 duly flew to Römpötti on 1 August, followed a week later by 1/LeLv 24. Their role was to prevent Soviet aircraft from flying over the western areas of the gulf, but the latter chose to fly under the protection of the anti-aircraft artillery at Oranienbaum instead, thus preventing any large-scale encounters.

Nonetheless, engagements did indeed take place, the first of which occurred on 6 August when 1/LeLv 24 downed two I-16s near Seiskari. Six days later 4/LeLv 24 claimed an Il-2 and an I-16 over Tolli lighthouse, whilst that evening 3/LeLv 26 leader 1Lt Puhakka led his Fiat *Schwarm* on a raid to Kronstadt, where they bounced four I-16s and downed them all. This sweep violated the unit's area of operations, and LeLv 26 was subsequently ordered to stay on the eastern side of the Karelian Isthmus.

Much of LeLv 24's intelligence on their counterparts' activities were

**4/LeLv 24 leader 1Lt Iikka Törrönen is strapped into BW-380 at Römpötti in early October 1942. Behind him, BW-377 taxies past, this aircraft being the mount of Sgt Tapio Järvi. Törrönen had claimed 11 kills by the time he was lost in action in this fighter on 2 May 1943. Järvi fought to the end of hostilities, scoring 28.5 victories (*SA-kuva*)**

The very last Brewster fighter of
HLeLv 24, BW-374 is seen at
Suulajärvi on 8 May 1944 – the date
on which it was picked up by a pilot
from HLeLv 26. During its time with
the former unit, the fighter was
successfully flown by 2/LeLv 24's
2Lt Eero Riihikallio, who claimed 4.5
kills with it during the bitter aerial
clashes of April-May 1943 (SA-kuva)

derived from an excellently placed forward observation post at Ino, where 'spotters' could actually see aircraft taking off from Kronstadt and Oranienbaum! New tactics were suitably employed to enact upon this information, the Brewsters being sent out to await the return of the Soviet formations. On 14 August the Finns claimed nine Hurricanes in two combats, and 48 hours later 3/LeLv 24 engaged a formation of aircraft late in the afternoon, Capt Karhunen (in BW-388) leading the attack;

'I was leading a six-plane Brewster flight on an interception mission. South of Seiskari I spotted an enemy formation of 8 SBs, 3 MiGs and 16 I-16s, which was flying at a height of 200 m. We attacked the fighter escort, and whilst the I-16s chose to fight, the others fled. In my first dive I shot down the I-16 at the extreme left of the formation, the aircraft diving into the sea. My second I-16 crashed into the water on fire, turning over as it hit. My third I-16 had just evaded the fire from another Brewster when I hit it with several bursts, the fighter then pulling up and being struck again, before falling into the sea wing first. I made 12 attacks.

'The escort flew at the same altitude as the SBs, and although the I-16 pilots fought bravely, they failed to use their numerical strength to pull up on the bombers' flanks and hit us from above.'

The Brewster pilots claimed 11 I-16s from 4.GIAP, KBF (guard's fighter aviation regiment of the Red Banner Baltic Fleet), whilst the 'MiGs' encountered were actually Il-2s from 57.AP, KBF.

On 18 August the largest combat of the summer occurred when information was received that 'ten' I-16s had been spotted near Tytärsaari heading eastwards. 1Lt Hans Wind scrambled with eight Brewsters at 2000 and flew to Seiskari to await the Russians' arrival. However, upon sighting the enemy, it was realised that there were nearer to 60 aircraft inn the formation, so Capt Karhunen and 1Lt Lumme both immediately departed with their Brewster Schwarmes to offer further assistance. Piloting BW-393, Wind described the resulting melee in his report;

'I engaged four Hurricanes with eight Brewsters, and after a short chase

1/LeLv 24 Brewster BW-371 is serviced at Suulajärvi in June 1943. The aircraft boasts a captured Russian 1000 hp M-63 engine which was fitted for trials purposes, although this was soon replaced by a trusty Cyclone unit. WO Viktor Pyötsiä was assigned this aircraft at the time of its re-engining, although he failed to score any victories with it (*V Lakio*)

I set one alight with two bursts. It fell into the forest in flames. Then about 60 I-16s appeared on the scene, and I quickly caused one to smoke before another I-16 succeeded in shooting a cannon shell through my port wing (two inches outboard of the wing tank). After pulling up I saw the I-16 that I had just fired at burning on the water's surface. I then fired at three I-16s in a series of head-on passes, but failed to see the results.

'Towards the end of the combat I managed to conveniently manoeuvre myself in behind a lone I-16, and the aircraft caught fire after my first burst and crashed into the sea.'

For the loss of just one pilot, the Finns claimed two Pe-2s, one Hurricane and 13 I-16s destroyed, Wind, Karhunen and Juutilainen each being credited with three kills. The Soviets officially lost at least a Yak-1 and LaGG-3 from 21.IAP, KBF and two I-16s from 71.IAP, KBF.

## OTHER FRONTS

LeLv 32 transferred to Nurmoila, on the Olonets Isthmus, during late May 1942, their Curtiss Hawks often being engaged in fierce fights with small formations flying more modern aircraft like the Pe-2, MiG-3 and LaGG-3 – all of which were much faster than the Hawk.

One such action took place on 5 September when WO Koskinen (in CU-551) and his wingman observed an unusually large formation of 35 - 40 aircraft over the River Svir at Lotinanpelto at noon. He duly radioed for help, and Capt Bremer scrambled with his *Schwarm*. In the following battle, which lasted a full hour, the Finns claimed four LaGG-3s, four I-16s (from 524.IAP), two MiG-3s and one Pe-2 all without losses.

During the first nine months on the Olonets, the Hawk pilots claimed 65 aircraft destroyed without loosing a single fighter in combat. With the

arrival of winter, flying on both sides of the front was done only as a matter of necessity, and if the weather permitted.

The 'ace race' had not yet started, and a more important target at that point was the Mannerheim Cross, which was had so far been awarded to pilots with 20 aerial victories – this was raised to 30 in 1943. By the end of 1942 the Continuation War ace list was as follows;

| Rank | Name | Squadron | Victories |
| --- | --- | --- | --- |
| WO | Juutilainen, Ilmari | 24 | 34 |
| WO | Tuominen, Oiva | 26 | 23 |
| Capt | Karhunen, Jorma | 24 | 22.5 |
| 2Lt | Nissinen, Lauri | 24 | 20.5 |
| WO | Kinnunen, Eero | 24 | 15.5 |
| 1Lt | Tervo, Kalevi | 32 | 15 |
| Maj | Luukkanen, Eino | 24 | 14.5 |
| 1Lt | Wind, Hans | 24 | 14.5 |
| SSgt | Katajainen, Nils | 24 | 13 |
| 1Lt | Pekuri, Lauri | 24 | 12.5 |
| Capt | Puhakka, Olli | 26 | 11 |
| WO | Koskinen, Eino | 32 | 11 |
| MSgt | Lehtovaara, Urho | 28 | 11 |
| 1Lt | Kokko, Pekka | 24 | 10 |

Of these pilots, Nissinen was tutoring at the cadet school, Luukkanen had been posted to command a recce squadron, Katajainen was flying anti-submarine aircraft and Kokko had become a test pilot. On the aircraft front, only the Brewsters were considered to have any potential life left, for the Fiats and Moranes were worn out – they could barely reach a top speed of 350 km/h – and the Hawk ranks were getting very thin.

Finland had tried in vain to purchase Messerschmitts early on in the conflict, and their persistence finally paid off when in late 1942 Germany agreed to sell them 30 Bf 109G-2s to equip one squadron, and cover any

The mount of leading Finnish ace WO 'Illu' Juutilainen during his time with 3/LeLv 24, BW-364 is seen parked on the hardstanding at Immola in May 1943. Its pilot scored no fewer than 28 kills with this aircraft between July 1941 and November 1942, the fin of 'orange 4' showing Juutilainen's overall score at that time to be 36 – the remaining kills were scored either with other Brewsters or on D.XXIs during the Winter War. Juutilainen left this aircraft behind when he was posted to the 'elite' LeLv 34 on 8 February 1943 (*Finnish Aviation Museum*)

This aircraft (BW-393) was the mount of Finland's second ranking ace, and 3/LeLv 24 leader, 1Lt 'Hasse' Wind, who is seen preparing to take-off in it at Suulajärvi on 12 September 1943. There are 33 victory bars painted on the fin of 'orange 9', Wind scoring 26.5 of this total in BW-393 between January 1942 and September 1943. His final haul in Brewsters reached 39, and he followed this up with 36 in Bf 109Gs for a total of 75 victories in 302 missions (*SA-kuva*)

attrition – a contract for these fighters was signed on 1 February 1943.

Just over a week prior to contracts being exchanged LeLv 34 was established at Immola on 23 January 1943, and ex-LeLv 32 commander, Maj Ehrnrooth, appointed to head the new squadron. The new squadron was intended to be a 'crack outfit' right from the start, with air force commander Maj-Gen Lundquist giving Ehrnrooth the authorisation to pick the best pilots from any of the Finnish fighter units. Despite bitter protests from other squadron commanders, LeLv 34 was duly formed.

Those pilots selected were duly sent to Germany for familiarisation on the Bf 109G, the Luftwaffe training officer placed in charge of the conversion initially insisting on a full-scale training programme as was taught to *ab initio Jagdflieger*. However, upon seeing the skill of the Finnish pilots, he agreed to a much shorter course. On 9 March 1943 the first 16 Bf 109G-2s left for Finland, followed by a second batch of 14 on 10 May.

The Bf 109G (and LeLv 34) scored its debut kill on 24 March when Capt Ervi and WO Juutilainen of 1/LeLv 34 intercepted a Pe-2 returning from a photo-reccce sortie over the Gulf of Finland. At 1430 Juutilainen, in MT-212, sent the bomber down near Suursaari.

## EASTERN KARELIAN EPISODE

Finnish intelligence at Tiiksjärvi discovered in early 1943 that the Soviets were building up a sizeable partisan training and supply base at Ieljärvi, some 50 km from the frontline. The Finns decided to destroy this complex before it could be made operational in the coming summer, duly despatching a single battalion of troops on skis to wipe out the target, supported by air cover from Tiiksjärvi-based MS.406s from LeLv 14.

On 16 March the Finns attacked Ieljärvi, and Capt Tainio of 1/LeLv 14 led six Moranes on aerial protection duties. Ten I-15bis of 839.IAP

The mechanic assigned to WO Juutilainen's BW-364 was Paavo Janhunen, and he is seen here sitting on its tailplane at Suulajärvi in April 1943. Although its former pilot had scored his last Brewster kill (in BW-351) on 23 November 1942, the fighter was still wearing Juutilainen's victory bars come the following spring. It was assigned to 1Lt Martti Salovaara upon Juutilainen's transfer out of 3/LeLv 24. Note the skull and crossbones painted onto the white distemper forward of the fin

LeLv 24 aces pose for the camera at Suulajärvi on 7 May 1943. They are, from left to right, 1st flight leader 1Lt 'Hasse' Wind (75 victories), WO 'Pappa' Turkka (17 victories) and 3rd flight leader Capt 'Joppe' Karhunen (31 victories). The men are grouped around the tail of Karhunen's BW-366, and the dog, named Peggy Brown, was also his (*SA-kuva*)

LeLv 34 commander Maj Eino Luukkanen taxies out for take-off in his personal Bf 109G-2 MT-201 at Utti on 1 June 1943. He claimed nine victories in this fighter out of a total of 56 in 441 missions. On 18 June 1944 Luukkanen was awarded the Mannerheim Cross (*ECPA*)

duly responded to the raid by attempting to strafe the Finnish troops, but they were repelled by the MS.406 pilots, who downed five fighters during the first assault and another two in a second attack. Future ace Sgt Hemmo Leino (in MS-319) was the most successful pilot, claiming two.

The base was duly destroyed once aerial superiority had been achieved

MT-216 was assigned to 3/LeLv 34 pilot MSgt Onni Paronen, and it is seen here after taxying into MT-213 at Utti on 20 May 1943 . Paronen flew 316 missions and was credited with 12.5 confirmed victories, whilst his fighter scored 12 kills also, although none of these were credited to Paronen (*Finnish War Archives*)

## BALTIC FLEET OFFENSIVE

In an attempt to stop Soviet submarines entering the Baltic Sea come the spring thaw in 1943, the Germans had used the cover of the winter weather to lay a double anti-submarine net across the Gulf of Finland from Porkkala to Naissaari, in Estonia. As a further anti-submarine measure, a double mine belt further east between Kotka and Narva had also been sown at the same time. To keep these protective boundaries operable, equipment and men were shuttled between the island 'links in the chain', with servicing vessels based at a northern supply base at Kotka. For over a year these supply points, and bases along the belt, became the prime target of the Red Banner Baltic Fleet air force. At around this time the air arm also started exchanging its I-153s and I-16s for La-5s and Yak-1s/-7s, as well as increasing numbers of Pe-2s and Il-2s. Better aircraft, allied with better tactical training, made the Russians more dangerous opponents.

The Soviet offensive commenced as soon as the sea was free of ice, LeLv 24 being given the responsibility of protecting the area. On 18 April it fought the first major air battle of the campaign 1Lt Lumme (in BW-370) leading seven Brewsters scrambled at 1700, with a further seven following five minutes, led by 1Lt Savonen (in BW-375). They intercepted eight Il-

2s (7.GShAP, KBF) and 50 fighters (21.IAP, KBF) west of Kronstadt, and in an hour-long combat claimed two Il-2s and 18 fighters destroyed.

On 21 April all three Brewster flights intercepted 35 Yak-1, LaGG-3 and La-5 fighters in the Seiskari-Kronstadt area. Leading the Finns into action were Capts Karhunen, Törrönen and Sarvanto, and for the cost of one Brewster shot down by fighters and another by Oranienbaum's flak, the Finns claimed 19 destroyed – both 4.GIAP and 21.IAP (both Red Banner Baltic Fleet units) are known to have suffered casualties.

Battles continued into May, and after six weeks of action, the obsolete Brewsters had claimed 81 aircraft destroyed for the loss of three in combat. These startling successes were achieved primarily by attacking from altitude, thus allowing 'pendulum' tactics to be employed.

On 21 May the Bf 109Gs had scored four kills in their first two encounters in-theatre, although in the latter engagement MT-228 had collided with an 1-153 of 71.IAP, KBF. 1Lt T Saalasti was killed in the crash, although Soviet pilot, Lt V Sitvinikov, managed to take to his parachute. The final encounter of the day took place at 1845 when Maj Luukkanen (MT-201) led 11 Bf 109Gs to the Seiskari-Lavansaari area to intercept four Il-2s (7.GShAP, KBF), escorted by 17 LaGG-3s and Yak-1s (13.IAP, KBF). Two of each type were reportedly downed, although Soviet records actually show the loss of an additional Il-2 and LaGG-3.

On 1 August 1943 LeLv 34 moved to the new Kymi airfield, just north of Kotka, thus expanding its area of responsibility to the Viipuri-Oranienbaum line in the east. This left the old Brewsters with far fewer opportunities for combat, and an increased chance of survival.

1/LeLv 34 pilots relax between sorties at Utti on 1 June 1943, although they have kept their lifejackets on in case of an emergency scramble. They are, from left to right, 1Lt Väinö Pokela (5 victories), MSgt Mauno Fräntilä (5.5 victories), WO Oiva Tuominen (44 victories), 1Lt Kalevi Tervo (23 victories), SSgt Gösta Lönnfors (1 victory) and SSgt Urho Lehto (3 victories). Parked behind them is MT-212, which was assigned to WO Ilmari Juutilainen – he had scored his first Messerschmitt kill (a Pe-2) in this fighter on 24 March 1943 (*ECPA*)

The final great air battles over the eastern Gulf of Finland prior to the onset of winter were fought on 23 September 1943. At 1330 four Brewsters of 3/LeLv 24, escorted by four Bf 109Gs from 1/LeLv 34, engaged against 20 aircraft from 4.GIAP, KBF in the vicinity of Shepelevskij lighthouse – three Yakovlevs and five Lavochkins were claimed to have been shot down. Two-and-a-half hours later, 1Lt Wind's seven Brewsters attacked 15 aircraft returning to Seiskari airfield, and claiming one Il-2 (7.GShAP, KBF) and six Lavochkins destroyed.

The 'ace race' was now in full swing, although WO Juutilainen was still clearly ahead. As of 31 December 1943, the list was as follows;

| Rank | Name | Squadron | Victories |
|------|------|----------|-----------|
| WO | Juutilainen, Ilmari | 34 | 53 |
| Capt | Wind, Hans | 24 | 38 |
| WO | Tuominen, Oiva | 34 | 31 |
| Maj | Luukkanen, Eino | 34 | 26.5 |
| Maj | Karhunen, Jorma | 24 | 26.5 |
| MSgt | Lehtovaara, Urho | 34 | 23.5 |
| 1Lt | Tervo, Kalevi | 34 | 23 |
| 1Lt | Nissinen, Lauri | 24 | 22.5 |
| Capt | Puhakka, Olli | 34 | 22 |
| 1Lt | Karhila, Kyösti | 34 | 19 |
| WO | Kinnunen, Eero | 24 | 19 |

On 14 February 1944 all frontline units received a prefix denoting their duty. Thus, instead of being just plain *Lentolaivues* (aviation, or flying, squadrons), the units became *Hävittäjälentolaivues* (fighter aviation squadrons), as follows;

LeLv 24 became HLeLv 24 (LeR 3)
LeLv 26 became HLeLv 26 (LeR 3)
LeLv 28 became HLeLv 28 (LeR 2)
LeLv 30 became HLeLv 30 (LeR 5)
LeLv 32 became HLeLv 32 (LeR 1)
LeLv 34 became HLeLv 34 (LeR 3)

## ─── BALTIC FLEET STRIKES KOTKA ───

Early in 1944 the Red Banner Baltic Fleet air force switched targets from the mine belt across the Gulf of Finland to the city of Kotka, and its port, or, on occasion, Hamina port, 20 km further east. This tactical change was made in an effort to disrupt the shipping of supplies to the front.

On 6 March Kotka experienced its first major air raid, resulting in Maj Luukkanen (in MT-201) scrambling with five Bf 109Gs at 1345. They subsequently intercepted a 40-aircraft formation over Narvi and shot down five Pe-2s from 12.GPBAP (guard's dive-bomber aviation regiment), KBF and two La-5s. Two-and-a-half hours later 1Lt Myllylä (in MT-216 )led five Bf 109Gs against a smaller formation, sending four aircraft down south of Kotka.

The following month saw the Finnish Air Force take receipt of enough new Bf 109G-6s to re-equip both HLeLv 30 and 34, the latter unit passing on its surviving G-2 to HLeLv 24.

1/LeLv 34 pilot SSgt Eino Peltola was assigned MT-215, which is seen here in a hangar at Helsinki Malmi in May 1943. Having scored 7.5 kills in Brewsters, Peltola had added a further three to his tally in Bf 109s (none in this particular aircraft, however) when he was shot down and killed in MT-226 on 2 April 1944 (*A Donner*)

On the morning of 17 May HLeLv 34 employed its new fighters rather differently than from before when it intercepted intruders heading for Kotka or Hamina. Instead of first climbing above the Soviet aircraft prior to attacking them, they now chose to hit them directly from below. This switch surprised the enemy, Maj Luukkanen's 11 Bf 109G-6s downing eight (of 27) Pe-2s from 12.GPBAP, KBF before their 15-strong escort could react. In the resulting melee, three Yaks were exchanged for one Bf 109.

WO Juutilainen piloted MT-222 with 1/LeLv 34 for ten months until 10 March 1944, when it was lost whilst being flown by another pilot – during this time he had scored 17 victories with it. 'Yellow 2' was photographed parked next to Douglas DC-2 *Hanssin Jukka* at Helsinki Malmi in late May 1943 (*A Donner*)

Capt Puhakka (in MT-419) was one of those to score;

'Right after take-off I saw a bomber formation of 10+, escorted by around 20 fighters, approaching Kotka. Before entering the interception area the planes turned east, having obviously observed the take-off of our fighters. I could not make it above the fighters, so I decided to attack the bombers from below. This tactic worked well, for I caught them as they pulled up and levelled off after diving at targets in the harbour.

'The first one I fired at burst into flames and dived into the sea just off Hamina. Utilising my speed advantage, I quickly fired at a second bomber, which also burst into flames and turned over into a dive. I did not have time to see where it crashed, however, although several large pieces came off the plane, including the canopy, and I saw one man bail out, although I did not observe a parachute.

'I then attacked a third bomber. Pieces soon fell off it, and the pilot entered a shallow dive and crashed into the sea between two small islands. I saw one man bail out, but did not observe if his parachute opened.'

On 19 May 1Lt Myllylä (in MT-406) scrambled from Kotka with nine Bf 109Gs when 20 Pe-2s of 12.GPBAP, escorted by 15 Yak-9s, were reported heading for the city. The Finns destroyed two bombers and four fighters as they chased them back to Lavansaari. This marked the end of the raids, for the Red air forces now began concentrating on *Generalissimus* Stalin's 'fourth strategic blow' – the assault on the Karelian Isthmus.

# SOVIET OFFENSIVE OF 1944

Following their successes on the German front in 1943-44, the Soviet Red Army carried out the fourth of its ten strategic attacks, and it proved to be the only one which failed to reach its goal.

Late May and early June 1944 saw Russian troop concentrations northwest of Leningrad substantially increase in size, as did the number of tanks and artillery pieces observed by Finnish reconnaissance aircraft. Unfortunately senior Finnish military figures failed to appreciate the seriousness of the sightings emanating from the fighter recce pilots.

The forthcoming 'Great Attack', as it became known in Finland, would see Soviet forces advancing in a 20-km wide ''wedge'' across the Gulf of Finland, supported by no fewer than 1300 aircraft from the 13th Air Army. A further 220 aircraft from the Red Banner Baltic Fleet air force were charged with covering the invading army's left flank.

Opposing this massive air armada on the Karelian Isthmus, *Lentorykmentti 3* could muster just 14 Bf 109G-2s from HLeLv 24, 16 Bf 109G-6s from HLeLv 34 and 18 Brewsters from HLeLv 26.

The attack commenced on 9 June, and after quickly breaking through the Finns' first defensive line, the Red Army soon had its enemy beating a hasty retreat. Within ten days the invasion spearhead had reached the outskirts of Viipuri, and following the capture of the city the next day, the Soviet advance was stopped so the communists could consolidate their newly-won gains. The first day of the offensive had seen the Red air forces fly some 1150 sorties, followed by another 800 the following day. Day

2/HLeLv 24's MT-227 is seen at Suulajärvi on 12 May 1944. It was then assigned to deputy flight leader 1Lt Urho Sarjamo, who had scored five kills with it prior to his death in action on 17 June 1944. He was shot down whilst flying this aircraft, and in one of the great tragedies of the war, the shattered remains of MT-227 crashed into MT-229, flown by 32.3-kill ace 1Lt Nissinen. The latter pilot was also killed outright. Sarjamo's score stood at 12.5 (from 334 missions) at the time of his death (*SA-kuva*)

2/HLeLv 24 pilot 1Lt Jorma 'Jotte' Saarinen sits strapped into the cramped cockpit of his Bf 109G in May 1944. Coming to the Messerschmitt with five victories already scored in Brewsters, he would rack up a further 18 kills in the German fighter, raising his total to 23 in 139 missions. Saarinen had the unenviable distinction of being the last Finnish fighter pilot killed in action, losing his life whilst attempting to force-land a shot-up MT-478 on 18 July 1944 (*SA-kuva*)

two of the invasion also saw the Finnish fighter force score its first victories when its pilots downed 16 aircraft during five separate encounters. On 14 June a further 18 were claimed in seven engagements, and three days later 21 fell in seven clashes.

On 19 June the arrival of new attrition replacement Bf 109G-6s from Germany made good the losses suffered by the fighter units up to this point in the battle, allowing both HLeLv 24 and 34 to reach almost full strength (25 aircraft). That same afternoon, a further two encounters resulted in six Soviet aircraft being destroyed. Finally, at 2000 an eight-aircraft formation from 3/HLeLv 34, led by Capt Puhakka, and ten Bf 109Gs from 3/HLeLv 24, commanded by Capt Wind, intercepted several regiments of Russian aircraft near Viipuri. The Finns destroyed six Pe-2s (58.BAP), three Airacobras (196.IAP), two Il-4s (836.BAP) and two La-5s (401.IAP), all for no loss. WO Lehtovaara, flying MT-406, claimed four aircraft during this epic engagement;

'I was part of a reconnaissance mission sent to patrol the route to Vammelsuu-Haapakangas-Kyyrölä. Soon after take-off I spotted about 30 enemy aircraft above Säkkijärvi, heading north, followed moments later by a further 20 machines. Other enemy formations also started to appear from the south-east, and SSgt Nuorala and I engaged in combat with enemy fighters over the Gulf of Viipuri.

'I eventually got into position to fire at two Airacobras from below and behind, one of which fell about four kilometres west of Koivisto and the other eight kilometres south-east of Koivisto. This engagement had taken up so much time that I could not continue my briefed reconnaissance mission, so I turned back to base. After flying south of Viipuri, I saw several Pe-2s, escorted by ten fighters, to the south-east of the city. I attacked, and managed to shoot at two of the Pe-2s from directly astern, causing both of then to burst into flames. The first came down about two kilometres south of Kämärä, and the second a further kilometre away.'

The air war reached its peak on 20 June when Russians troops forced their way into the streets of Viipuri, supported by a massive aerial 'umbrella' of fighters and ground attack aircraft. Before midday, the Finnish Bf 109G pilots had already been embroiled in three large-scale actions which had seen them claim 35 aircraft shot down. Before the end

SSgt Tapio 'Tappi' ('Shorty') Järvi scored all his kills with 2/HLeLv 24. Seen here in May 1944, he had achieved 11.5 victories in Brewsters prior to tallying a further 17 in Messerschmitts in 1944, raising his final total to 28.5 in 247 missions (*SA-kuva*)

2/HLeLv 24's MT-213 is run up seconds prior to commencing its take-off roll at Suulajärvi on 12 May 1944. This fighter was one of just a handful of Bf 109Gs that actually had its Luftwaffe 'greys' oversprayed with the standard Finnish black/green camouflage scheme. During the Soviet summer offensive of 1944, MT-213 was flown by 1Lt Eero Riihikallio, who claimed a total of 16.5 victories (three in this aircraft) in 110 missions (*SA-kuva*)

1/HLeLv 34 ace SSgt Erik Lyly admires his unit's new emblem (a fledgling eagle) painted on the tail of MT-423. Based on an idea put forward by the squadron CO, the emblem was officially adopted on 7 June 1944. Lyly scored eight victories in 188 missions (*E Lyly*)

Another photograph of Bf 109G-6 MT-423 at Kymi in June 1944. It was then assigned to 1/HLeLv 34 pilot SSgt Hemmo Leino, who had become an ace on 10 October 1943. Leino had scored victories with LeLv 30's D.XXIs and LeLv 14's MS.406s before achieving further successes in the Messerschmitt. His final total was 11 kills (one in this fighter) in 251 missions (*Finnish Aviation Museum*)

of the day a further five battles had taken place, the Finns claiming an additional 16 victories to bring total victories for the 20th to a staggering 51 – 31 to HLeLv 24 and 20 to HLeLv 34. Multiple losses were suffered by the Yak-9-equipped 14.GIAP, the La-5-manned 159.IAP, Airacobra unit 196.IAP and the Il-2-equipped 943. and 35.ShAP, KBF.

The Finnish pilots scored a further ten kills the next day, followed by 14 on the 22nd, 28 on the 23rd, 20 on the 26th, 44 on the 28th and 12 on the 29th. To cap off an extraordinary month, 30 June saw WO Juutilainen become the second Finn to achieve 'ace in a mission' status;

Fully kitted out in late war flying gear, 1/HLeLv 24's aces pose for a group shot at Suulajärvi in April 1944. They are, from left to right, 1Lt Mikko Pasila (10 victories), WO Viktor Pyötsiä (19.5 victories), flight leader 1Lt Lauri Nissinen (32.5 victories), 2Lt Heimo Lampi (13.5 victories), 1Lt Kai Metsola (10.5 victories) and Sgt Arvo Koskelainen (5 victories). Behind them is Nissinen's MT-225 (*V Lakio*)

3/HLeLv 24 aces present a far less 'uniform' sight in respect to their apparel at Lappeenranta in July 1944. They are, from left to right, flight leader 1Lt Kyösti Karhila (32 kills), squadron CO Maj Jorma Karhunen (31 kills), the father of 1Lt Ahti Laitinen (10 victories) who had been made a PoW on 29 June 1944,

'We were on a combat air patrol with eight aircraft over Tali when we met enemy fighters. I hit one Airacobra in the upper rear fuselage and the majority of its tail flew off, causing it to crash on the Torkkeli park side of the Red Spring market place, trailing flaming fuel in its wake. The battle then continued towards Säiniö, where I managed to hit another Airacobra from above and behind, causing it to crash between Säiniö and Karhusuo.

'I then spotted 50+ bombers approaching from the east, escorted by fighters. I assembled my flight between Juustila and Tali, and then dived

1Lt Atte Nyman (5 victories), SSgt Emil Vesa (29.5 victories), SSgt Leo Ahokas (12 victories) and Sgt Kosti Koskinen (2 victories). Behind them is Vesa's Bf 109G, MT-460 (*SA-kuva*)

1/HLeLv 34 pilots 1Lt Ilmari Joensuu (five victories) and SSgt Kauko Tuomikoski (four victories) pose in front of MT-416 at Kymi in May 1944. Joensuu was 195 cm tall, and so was appropriately nicknamed 'Pitkä-Jim' ('Long Jim') (*K Tuomikoski*)

'Yellow 6' MT-416 was photographed on the point of take-off at Taipalsaari in late June 1944. Assigned to 3/HLeLv 34 (as denoted by the tactical number on its fin), the fighter was often flown by SSgt Aaro Nuorala. A successful Messerschmitt pilot, he scored ten kills (six in MT-416) with the German fighter to add to three victories in D.XXIs with LeLv 30 in 1941-42 and 1.5 kills flying MS.406s with LeLv 14 in 1943. Nuorala completed 250 missions (*K Risku*)

into the enemy. Over Juustila I downed a Yak-9, which crashed in flames, whilst a second Yak-9 was destroyed in the same area after I shot its starboard wing off.

'We then provided an escort for German Stukas, after which we again came into contact with Russian fighters and bombers. This time I failed to achieve any conclusive results, so I turned my attentions instead towards a formation of Il-2s, and their escorts. I then spotted some Il-2s devoid of fighter protection, so I quickly manoeuvred into them from side-on and shot an Il-2 down in flames over the Juustila peninsula. At the same time I was effectively surrounded by a vastly superior number of La-5 escorts. After "wrestling" with them for five minutes, I managed to shoot one down in flames from an altitude of 2000 m, the La-5 crashing 3-4 km north of the Il-2 alongside a road.

'I then ran out of the ammunition, so I had to break off the fight. Frustratingly, I still had ten minutes of fuel left.'

Juutilainen was subsequently credited with six victories, two of which were deemed to be personal scores and the remaining four regimental kills. During this mission, flown between 1045 and 1200, HLeLv 34 despatched eight Bf 109Gs and HLeLv 24 seven, and between them they

3/HLeLv 34's MT-445 was photographed in late September 1944 after its yellow axis identification markings had been stripped off. This aircraft was one of just 14 G-6/R6 'gun-boats' delivered to the Finns with underwing 20 mm cannon fitted. On 20 June 1944 it was assigned to SSgt Klaus 'Santtu' Alakoski, who shot down eight aircraft with it, although by then the cannon had been removed in order to improve the fighter's manoeuvrability. Alakoski ended the war with 26 kills from 239 missions

MT-451 'gunboat' belonged to 1/HLeLv 34, and is seen at Taipalsaari in July 1944, again with the wing cannon removed. On 5 August 1944 squadron CO, Maj Eino Luukkanen, scored the unit's last kill flying this aircraft when he downed a Yak-9 over the Gulf of Finland (*K Risku*)

claimed 15 aircraft destroyed out of 200-300 observed – 404.IAP is known to have lost Yak-9s, 403.IAP P-39s and 872.ShAP Il-2s.

## AIRFIELD STRIKES

Both HLeLv 24's base at Lappeenranta and HLeLv 34's airfield at Taipalsaari had escaped Soviet attention throughout June, as had the German-held Immola site. However, on the evening of 2 July 35 Pe-2s and 40 Il-2s, escorted by 20 fighters, attacked Lappeenranta. Fortunately radio intelligence alerted HLeLv 24 of the imminent raid, allowing the unit to get 11 freshly refuelled and re-armed Bf 109Gs airborne. However, some could not be made airworthy in time, and two valuable Messerschmitt fighters were duly destroyed and four more damaged. Two captured Pe-2s reconnaissance aircraft from PLeLv 48 were also burnt out.

Eight Bf 109Gs from Taipalsaari also scrambled in response to the raid, arriving over the airfield just five minutes after taking off. They quickly cut a swathe through the ranks of the vulnerable Il-2, and together with HLeLv 24, claimed 11 shot down from 448, 703 and 872.ShAP (all members of 281.ShAD). A further four Pe-2s and a solitary Yak-9 were also claimed to have been destroyed.

Despite the ferocity of the airfield attacks, neither the Finns at Lappeenranta or the *Gefechtsverband Kuhlmey* at Immola had their ability to undertake combat patrols seriously affected.

This was clearly illustrated less than 24 hours later when Finnish Bf 109G pilots reported the destruction of 21 aircraft, followed by a further 14 on the 5th. On 9 July the scoreboard showed ten kills, and the next day 13. These huge aerial melees reached a peak on the 15th when the Finns

3/HLeLv 24 Bf 109G MT-476 is readied for a sortie at Lappeenranta on 3 July 1944. It was briefly assigned to MSgt Nils Katajainen (35.5 victories), who was wounded in action after downing a Yak-9 in it two days later. He succeeded in crash-landing the stricken Messerschmitt, but subsequently spent many months in hospital recuperating. Passing behind MT-476 is MT-441, which was used by 1Lt Ahti Laitinen to score eight of his ten kills. His run of success in this fighter in late June came to abrupt halt on the 29th when he was shot down whilst flying Hans Wind's MT-439 and made a PoW (*SA-kuva*)

MT-465 belonged to 2/HLeLv 24, being was assigned to five-victory ace 1Lt Atte Nyman. It is seen here stripped off its wing cannon at Lappeenranta in July 1944. Note how the 2nd Flight placed its tactical number (in this case 'yellow 7') behind the cockpit (*A Nyman*)

HLeLv 34 was stationed at Lappeenranta between 16 and 23 June 1944, and during its brief time at the airfield the 1st Flight's MT-435 is seen at readiness with its pilot strapped in. This aircraft was not an 'ace's mount', although MSgt Antti Tani claimed a Yak-9 in it on 21 June 1944 for his 17th kill in a final tally of 21.5 (*H Leino*)

*1/HLeLv 34 'gun-boat' MT-453 was photographed against a Taipalsaari sunset during July 1944. It was assigned to SSgt Osmo Länsivaara, who almost 'made ace' with four victories. Antti Tani also used this fighter to down a trio of Il-2s on 1 July 1944 (K Tuomikoski)*

claimed 12 Soviet aircraft destroyed in five encounters. Staggeringly, these numbers could have been even higher had the Finnish fighter pilots not been so dedicated to the task of escorting the bombers of LeR 4. Indeed, so effective were the pilots in this role that not a single bomber was shot down by fighters whilst operating over the Karelian Isthmus.

Following a planned retreat, the Finns dug in between Tali and Ihantala, causing the the invasion across the Gulf of Viipuri to stall, before finally stopping altogether after the Soviet push between Vuosalmi and Äyräpää did not materialise. Stalin duly called off the offensive on 12 July after exhausting his reserves of troops, although bitter fighting continued along the new frontline for a further six days. A combination of the stiff rearguard action by the Finnish army and the successful Allied landings in Normandy early the previous month had a great influence on Stalin's decision to halt the invasion and focus instead on the push for Berlin.

The attack on the secondary front at Olonets Isthmus had commenced 12 days after the main offensive, and it too had been stopped well short of its original goal prior to it being abandoned on 17 July.

During the 38 days of the 'Great Attack', Bf 109G pilots claimed no fewer than 425 aircraft shot down and another 78 damaged during 355 missions (2168 sorties). In turn ten Messerschmitts were lost to Soviet fighters, three posted missing in action, three more to flak and two to 'assault' aircraft. Eight pilots were killed and three captured. The Luftwaffe's II./JG 54 claimed 126 aircraft in 179 missions (984 sorties) during the same period. Soviet losses were indeed heavy, for by the time fighting stopped on the Karelian Isthmus, the 13th Air Army possessed just 800 aircraft. The top scorers of the summer offensive of 1944 were;

| Rank | Name | Squadron | Victories |
| --- | --- | --- | --- |
| WO | Juutilainen, Ilmari | 34 | 34 |
| Capt | Wind, Hans | 24 | 33 |
| 1Lt | Puro, Olavi | 24 | 28.5 |
| Maj | Luukkanen, Eino | 34 | 22 |
| MSgt | Vesa, Emil | 24 | 20 |
| SSgt | Järvi, Tapio | 24 | 19 |
| 1Lt | Saarinen, Jorma | 24 | 18 |
| MSgt | Katajainen, Nils | 24 | 18 |

1/HLeLv 26 Brewsters at Mensu-vaara in July 1944. The aircraft in the foreground is BW-364, which had been used by 1Lt Teromaa to claim four kills the previous month. Following almost a three-year association with the Brewster fighter, Teromaa spent the final two months of the war in command of 2/HLeLv 24, with whom he claimed six kills in Bf 109Gs. He flew a total of 225 missions and scored 19 victories (*A Juurinen*)

1Lt Erik Teromaa is seen at Immola in mid-June 1944 whilst still in command of 1/HLeLv 26. He subsequently used the Brewster (BW-361) parked behind him to claim a German Ju 87 shot down over northern Finland on 3 October 1944, although this kill cannot be confirmed from German loss reports (*O Riekki*)

| 1Lt | Suhonen, Väinö | 24 | 16 |
| Sgt | Halonen, Eero | 24 | 16 |
| WO | Lehtovaara, Urho | 34 | 15 |
| SSgt | Alakoski, Klaus | 34 | 14 |
| 1Lt | Karhila, Kyösti | 24 | 13 |
| Capt | Puhakka, Olli | 34 | 11 |
| 1Lt | Myllylä, Paavo | 34 | 10 |
| 1Lt | Riihikallio, Eero | 24 | 10 |
| 1Lt | Teromaa, Erik | 26 and 24 | 10 |

## ARMISTICE

Having repelled their invasion, Finland now sought a permanent peace with the USSR, and this lead to an armistice on 4 September 1944 and the signing of a truce in Moscow two weeks later. Its terms included the removal of German troops from northern Finland, resulting in a short land war being fought in Lapland against their former ally. In February 1947 the truce was ratified in the Paris Peace Treaty, forcing Finland to hand over the same chunk of land as had been surrendered in 1940, plus the town of Petsamo on the Arctic Sea coast. These demands were hardly fair, for Soviet troops had never even got close to seizing either area.

During the two wars Finnish flying units officially claimed 1807 aircraft destroyed out of a total of 3313. Flak accounted for 1345, whilst the rest comprised aircraft downed by naval units, those destroyed on the ground (not those destroyed in Finnish bomber raids) or aircraft seen to crash whilst attempting to avoid Finnish fighters or flak. Fighters were also responsible for downing 28 observation and fire-control balloons.

In turn, the Finnish Air Force lost 257 aircraft on operations, 215 non-operationally and 100 in training accidents. Personnel losses amounted to 353 airmen killed or missing in action and 86 in flying accidents.

In respect to the accuracy of the pilots' claims, recent research in Russian files has revealed that 1855 aircraft were downed by Finnish fighters, with the aces themselves accounting for 77 per cent of this figure.

# TOP ACES

## Warrant Officer Eino Ilmari Juutilainen

Ilmari Juutilainen was born in Lieksa in eastern Finland on 21 February 1914. In 1935 he enlisted in the air force, and on 1 May 1937 was posted to LAs. 5 (Air Station 5) as a reconnaissance sergeant pilot. He subsequently retrained as a fighter pilot and was duly posted to the 3rd Flight of LLv 24, which was equipped with D.XXI, on 3 March 1939.

On 30 November 1939 the Winter War broke out, and in his first combat on 19 December 1939, 'Illu' Juutilainen downed a Tupolev SB. On the last day of the year, whilst flying FR-106, he claimed an I-16 and was also promoted to staff sergeant – 25 days later he had risen to the rank of master sergeant. During the Winter War he flew 115 missions. Juutilainen received his final promotion to a warrant officer on 1 March 1941.

The Continuation War started on 25 June 1941, and it found Juutilainen flying BW-364 in 3/LeLv 24. In his first combat on 9 July, he claimed two 'Chaikas' destroyed, whilst on 12 August he scored his first 'triple' – all I-153s, claimed in BW-364 during a single sortie. His second 'triple' came on 26 September in the same machine. On 26 April 1942 he was awarded the Mannerheim Cross (No 56) for scoring 20 victories, and on 18 August he claimed his third 'triple'. By the time he was posted to 1/LeLv 34 on 8 February 1943, his scoreboard showed 36 kills, all bar two having been scored in Brewsters during the course of 181 missions.

At his new unit, 'Illu' was initially assigned Bf 109G-2 MT-212, although this aircraft was lost when 44-kill ace WO Oiva Tuominen ditched after downing a Pe-2 on 2 June 1943. Juutilainen was subsequently given MT-222 as a replacement, and he scored a 'triple' with it three days later. 10 July saw a further three victories fall to the air force's ranking ace, although these were claimed in MT-217. On 27 October 1943 Juutilainen destroyed three La-5s, whilst on 6 March 1944 his 'triple' comprised two Pe-2s and a Yak-9 – all scored on single missions.

MT-426 was assigned to Juutilainen on 30 May 1944, and ten days later he again downed three aircraft in a single sortie, plus an Il-2 (flying MT-424) later that same day. On 20 June 'Illu' claimed five in three missions, and on the 26th scored a 'triple' in MT-422. Two days later he won the Mannerheim Cross for the second time after attaining 75 victories – he and Hans Wind were the first to achieve such an accolade. Indeed, this award was issued twice to just four Finnish soldiers.

Juutilainen was then assigned MT-457, and on 30 June he equalled Jorma Sarvanto's score of six on a single mission, being credited with two

1/HLeLv 34's WO Ilmari Juutilainen, photographed on 30 June 1944 (*SA-kuva*)

**3/LeLv 24 flight leader, 1Lt Hans Wind, on 31 July 1943 (*SA-kuva*)**

Yak-9s, two P-39s, one La-5 and one Il-2. The next day Juutilainen scored a 'triple' over two missions, and then repeated the feat on 5 July, but on a single sortie. On 3 September (just 24 hours before the armistice) Juutilainen claimed a Lisunov Li-2 transport, thus bringing his score to 94 victories in 437 missions – the highest non-German score in Europe.

On 16 May 1947 Juutilainen resigned from the air arm with a full pension. He bought a light aircraft and became a regular sight at various airshows for a decade until fully retiring. He is still alive and well in 1998.

## Captain Hans Henrik Wind

'Hasse' Wind was born on 30 July 1919 at Tammisaari. Upon graduation from the local secondary school, he was accepted into ISK (Air Fighting School) in 1939. The following year he went to cadet school and then joined LLv 25 (advanced training unit) on 16 June 1941 as a 1st lieutenant.

On 1 August 1941 Wind was posted firstly to 4/LeLv 24 and then to 1/LeLv 24, with whom he scored his first kill on 27 September 1941 – shared with Capt Eino Luukkanen. The New Year saw him back at 4/LeLv 24, where he became an ace on 29 March 1942 flying Brewster BW-378. On 1 August he joined 1/LeLv 24 as deputy flight leader, and two weeks later Wind downed two Hurricanes, followed on the 18th by two more Hurricanes and an I-16 – he used BW-393 on both missions.

On 7 November he assumed command of 1/LeLv 24 from Maj Eino Luukkanen, remaining in charge until Capt Jorma Sarvanto arrived on 16 January 1943. On 4 May Wind (again in BW-393) downed three Il-2s and an I-153 in a single sortie. This haul was followed up by a 'triple' 16 days later. On 27 May Wind was appointed CO of 3/LeLv 24, taking BW-393 with him. On 31 July he received the Mannerheim Cross (No 116), having taken his score to 34, and on 19 October he 'made' captain. Wind claimed his 39th, and last, Brewster kill on 21 March 1944 .

The following month HLeLv 24 converted to Bf 109Gs, and Wind was assigned MT-201. On 13 June he downed four Pe-2s in a single sortie flying this aircraft, the veteran G-2 (in which he had scored 11 kills in total) finally being replaced by G-6 MT-439 on 19 June 1944. Over the next ten days Wind used this machine to claim 25 aircraft destroyed, including hauls of five on the 20th from two sorties, four on the 23rd in a single sortie, and five again on both the 26th and 28th (both in two sorties).

During the second of the two sorties flown on 28 June, his cockpit was struck by a 20 mm shell soon after he had downed the third, and last, Yak-9 to fall to his guns during the course of the engagement. Although badly wounded, Wind nevertheless managed to get MT-439 safely back to Lappeenranta, and he was hospitalised for the rest of the war. That same day he was awarded the Mannerheim Cross for the second time. Wind had flown 302 missions and was credited with 75 victories.

Leaving active duty on 10 October 1945, he acquired a degree in economics, and went on to hold senior positions in the shoe and bakery industries before retiring in 1984. Hans Wind died on 24 July 1995.

## Major Eino Antero Luukkanen

Eino Luukkanen was born at Jaakkima, in Karelia, on 4 June 1909. In

1929 he volunteered for military service at Maalentokoulu (Land-based Aviation School) at Utti, graduating the following year and progressing to cadet school. Luukkanen completed his training in 1933 as a 2nd lieutenant, and was posted to LAs. 6. On 21 March 1935 he joined LAs. 5 (as a 1st lieutenant), where he flew Bulldogs.

On 24 January 1939 he was transferred to command 3/LLv 24, being D.XXI FR-104. On the second day of the Winter War he claimed an SB bomber over the Karelian Isthmus (the third victory for his squadron). Luukkanen's original fighter was damaged by ground fire soon after, and its replacement, FR-108, was used to claim a further 1.5 aircraft destroyed. On 15 February 1940 'Eikka' Luukkanen 'made' captain.

The start of the Continuation War found Luukkanen in command of 1/LeLv 24, flying Brewster BW-375. In his first combat on 8 July 1941, he claimed one 'Chaika' destroyed and another damaged – documentation has just been found confirming the latter did indeed crash. On 1 June 1942 he was assigned BW-393, and he used the fighter to score six kills up to 7 November 1942 – by which time

1/LeLv 24 commander, Maj Eino Luukkanen, on 7 November 1942 (*V Lakio*)

his tally had reached 17. By now a major, Luukkanen took command of LeLv 30, flying captured I-153s and D.XXIs in the maritime recce role.

On 29 March 1943 he was posted to lead the new LeLv 34, being issued with the first Bf 109G-2 (MT-201) delivered to Finland. Luukkanen scored steadily throughout the following year, and on 6 March 1944 achieved his first 'triple' by down two Pe-2 and an La-5. The following month his unit converted to the new G-6, and he was assigned MT-417. On 14 June he claimed three fighters and four days later he received the Mannerheim Cross (No 127). On the 19th he was downed by flak after destroying a fire-control balloon, belly landing in no-man's land.

Within 24 hours Luukkanen was back in action, using MT-415 to score a 'triple' on 23 June. Aside from numerous single kills, he claimed a further four 'doubles' up to 5 August, when he achieved his unit's final success of the war in MT-451 – a Yak-9 shot into the Gulf of Finland.

Luukkanen flew 441 sorties during his career, which was the highest number achieved by any Finnish fighter pilot. His final kill tally was 56.

**2/LeLv 28 pilot SSgt Urho Lehtovaara, seen on 9 September 1941 (*P Massinen*)**

Postwar, Luukkanen remained in command of his unit, which was redesignated HLeLv 33 on 4 December 1944. On 13 February 1948 he was promoted to lieutenant-colonel and given command of *Lentorykmentti* 2, based at Rissala. On 8 November 1951 he finally retired from the air force, Luukkanen then entering the timber trade, before dying prematurely on 10 April 1964.

## Warrant Officer Urho Sakari Lehtovaara

Lehtovaara was born on 27 October 1917 at Pyhäjärvi, in northern Finland. In 1937 he went into military service, and in 1939 was accepted for pilot training. On 10 February 1940 he was posted as a corporal to 2/LLv 28, scoring a kill with MS.406 MS-326 during the Winter War. Lehtovaara was promoted to sergeant on 23 March 1940.

The start of the Continuation War found Lehtovaara still with 2/LeLv 28, flying MS-327. Nicknamed 'Pikku-Jätti' ('Little Giant'), owing to his small build, Lehtovaara enjoyed his first success of the new conflict on 3 July 1941 when he downed a DB-3, and he followed this up six days later with two SBs and a MiG-3 in a single mission. On 23 July Lehtovaara downed two more DB-3s, and was then promoted to staff sergeant.

On 9 September he claimed three I-16s in a single sortie whilst flying MS-304, and two days later he was rewarded with promotion to master sergeant. Lehtovaara's unit then went to Karelia, where opportunities for further kills were scarce. On 5 March 1943 he claimed a 'double' as his last (of 15) victories in the Morane, before transferring 23 days later to 3/LeLv 34. Lehtovaara's first Bf 109G kills came on 19 April, and he steadily added to his score throughout the year whilst usually flying machines other than his personal MT-218.

On 6 March 1944 Lehtovaara (in MT-235) downed two Pe-2 in his first sortie of the day, and then destroyed an La-5 on the second. On 26 April he was promoted to a warrant officer. When the new Bf 109G-6s arrived shortly afterwards he was issued with MT-404, and he scored a 'double' with the fighter on 17 May. On 19 June Lehtovaara destroyed two Pe-2s and two P-39s (in MT-406) on a single sortie, whilst 2 July saw him chase more Pe-2s from Lappeenranta to Viipuri, where he destroyed three. Seven days later he was awarded the Mannerheim Cross (No 142).

On 25 July Lehtovaara claimed a P-39 as his last victory, which took his tally to 44.5 from 400+ missions. On 22 November 1946 he resigned from the air force, and eventually became a cinema manager, before also suffering a premature death on 5 January 1949.

## Warrant Officer Oiva Emil Kalervo Tuominen

'Oippa' Tuominen was born on 5 March 1908 in Kouvola in southern Finland. In 1926 he volunteered for military service at the air force's recruiting centre in Helsinki, and was duly trained as an aircraft mechanic. However, he wanted to fly, and in 1933 he was finally accepted into ISK and graduated as a sergeant pilot flying recce aircraft with LAs. 5. On 1 January 1938 he was posted to the Bulldog-equipped LLv 26.

Shortly before the outbreak of the Winter War, he was transferred to 1/LLv 24, equipped with D.XXIs , and subsequently scored 1.5 kills on type. On 30 January 1940 he was promoted to sergeant and sent back to 2/LLv 26, which was now equipped with Gladiators – Tuominen scored his first two kills with the Gloster fighter in GL-258 three days later. On 13 February he (in GL-255) and WO Lauri Lautamäki downed five SBs between them, Tuominen's share being 3.5 bombers destroyed. Later that same the day he claimed a Polikarpov R-5 just after he had taken off. His final score of eight during the Winter War placed him second in the overall ace listings for the conflict. On 25 April he was promoted to sergeant major.

Tuominen was serving with 1/LeLv 26 when the Continuation War erupted. On 4 July 1941, whilst flying Fiat G.50 FA-3 instead of 'his' FA-26, he claimed four SBs destroyed in one sortie. Nineteen days later he was promoted to warrant officer. On 18 August Tuominen became the first air force pilot to win the Mannerheim Cross (No 6), his accumulated score then standing at 20.

Tuominen remained with 1/LeLv 26 into 1943, his tally of 23 in Fiats including six 'doubles'. On 8

1/LeLv 26 pilot WO Oiva Tuominen points to his detailed scoreboard on G.50 FA-26 on 22 October 1942 (*V Salo*)

February 1943 he joined 1/LeLv 34, before moving four months later to 2/LeLv 34, where he was assigned Bf 109G-2 MT-220. His score continued to rise until 22 August, when his flight was transferred to Helsinki for city protection duties. On 6 March 1944 he joined HLeLv 30, but returned to 3/HLeLv 34 on 6 July and was thrust straight back into action in MT-405. Tuominen's last kill was claimed on 18 July 1944, and in his 400+ mission career, he was credited with 44 confirmed kills.

Tuominen resigned from the air force on 6 January 1945 and became a taxi driver in Helsinki. He kept up his flying skills, however, piloting light aircraft for almost 30 years. He died on 28 January 1976.

## Captain Risto Olli Petter Puhakka

Puhakka was born in Sortavala, Karelia, on 11 April 1916. In 1935 he graduated from secondary school and was accepted into the ISK for officer pilot training. He graduated on 6 October 1936 with the rank of 2nd lieutenant, but went to university to study law rather than to cadet school.

With the outbreak of the Winter War, he was posted to LLv 26, although he was duly attached to 1/LLv 24, with whom he flew D.XXIs (primarily FR-117). He scored four kills before being posted to the Fiat G.50-equipped 3/LLv 26 on 30 January 1940. On 15 February Puhakka was promoted to 1st lieutenant, and two weeks later he was given command of the flight after 1Lt Urho Nieminen was wounded in action. He had added a further two kills to his tally by the end of the Winter War.

Puhakka then spent time teaching at the cadet school, but by the time the Continuation War erupted on 25 June 1941, he was back with his old unit, 3/LeLv 26, flying G.50 FA-1. On 13 July Puhakka scored his first kills of the new conflict with a 'triple' haul, and within a month his tally had risen to an accumulated 12 kills from both wars. Following a tour as an instructor with various fighter squadrons that lasted until 3 June 1942, Puhakka then assumed command of 3/LeLv 26. Assigned G.50 FA-25, he scored a further five kills and 'made' captain on 29 December 1942.

On 9 February 1943 Puhakka became CO of the newly-formed 3/LeLv 34, being assigned Bf 109G-2 MT-204. Although he claimed just three kills in this fighter, he enjoyed success in other machines, and on 20 August he used MT-216 to down three La-5s and an Il-2 in two missions. On 17 May 1944 Puhakka destroyed a trio of Pe-2s in MT-419, followed exactly a month later by another 'triple' in the same fighter, although on this occasion he had to belly-land the battle-damaged Bf 109G.

Flying MT-433 for the remaining months of the war, Puhakka had flown 401 missions and claimed 42 victories – three of them without firing a shot – by the time of the ceasefire. On 21 December he was awarded the Mannerheim Cross (No 175). Generally considered to be the most skillful pilot in the fighter arm Puhakka resigned from the air force on 25 July 1946 and flew airliners, rising to the position of chief pilot prior to retirement at age 55 in 1971. On 28 January 1989 Puhakka passed away.

3/LeLv 26 leader 1Lt Olli Puhakka on 10 September 1942 (*SA-kuva*)

## 1st Lieutenant Olavi Kauko Puro

Olavi 'Olli' Puro was born on 18 November 1918 in Helsinki. After graduating from secondary school, he volunteered for military service in 1940, becoming a 2nd lieutenant on 11 February 1941. Trained as a pilot soon afterwards, he was posted firstly to LeLv 24 on 22 June 1942, before joining 3/LeLv 6 three months later, where he flew captured I-153s.

2/HLeLv 24 pilot 1Lt Lieutenant Olavi Puro seen in the cockpit of a Bf 109G on 1 July 1944 (*SA-kuva*)

Puro demonstrated his skills by downing two aircraft in IT-18 before returning to 2/LeLv 24 on 4 April 1943. He went on to down 5.5 aircraft during the great air battles of the following two months over the Gulf of Finland, flying Brewsters' BW-387 and BW-365.

On 19 October 1943 Puro was promoted to 1st lieutenant.

In May 1944 his flight converted to Bf 109Gs, and he was assigned MT-246, in which he scored 4.5 kills. On 20 June, while flying MT-201, he was credited with five victo-

ries in two missions, and three days later (in MT-449) he scored four in two missions. Puro was, however, wounded in the same battle at Hans Wind on 28 June 1944.

Returning to 2/HLeLv 24 on 9 July with one leg still in plaster, he scored four kills the following day during two missions in MT-479. On 22 July he scored a 'triple', and the following day he destroyed an La-5 for his 36th, and last, victory. Puro had flown 207 missions in total.

On 10 November 1944 he returned to civilian life and taught himself economics. Puro then went into banking, retiring in 1983 from the position of data processing director. Now aged 79, Puro is still alive and well.

## Master Sergeant Nils Edvard Katajainen

Katajainen was born in Helsinki on 31 May 1919. He was accepted into military service in 1939, joining the ISK and training as a fighter pilot. On 18 June 1941 Cpl 'Nipa' Katajainen was posted to 3/LeLv 24 and assigned Brewster BW-368. Ten days later he made his first kill, and duly became an ace as a sergeant on 12 August 1941 with the destruction of two 'Chaikas'. On 12 April 1942 he was promoted to staff sergeant.

Following his 13th kill, Katajainen was suddenly posted on 9 September 1942 to a training unit to learn the intricacies of flying twin-engined patrol aircraft, prior to joining LeLv 6 on 18 October 1942 – where he flew captured SBs on anti-submarine patrols! He soon applied to return to fighters, and finally on 9 April 1943 he was posted back to 3/LeLv 24, with whom he scored a further 4.5 kills. On 24 September 1943 he was promoted to master sergeant, and in April 1944 converted to Bf 109Gs.

Katajainen was subsequently wounded in combat on 2 June 1944, and although entitled to further recuperative leave, he returned to 3/HLeLv 24 on 21 June and recommenced his scoring run just two days by downing three kills in two sorties. On both 26 and 28 June he scored 'triples' in MT-436, whilst on 3 July he went one better with four aircraft in two missions, although his own Bf 109G (MT-462) was so badly shot up that he had to belly-land it. Two days later he destroyed a Yak-9, but was again wounded. This time he crash-landed MT-476 in a barely conscious state at Lappeenranta doing 500 km/h, and although destroying the fighter, Katajainen survived to recover in hospital. This time the war was over for him, however, his 196 sorties having realised 35.5 victories.

On 10 November 1944 Katajainen was released from service, and on 21 December he received the Mannerheim Cross (No 170) – the only fighter pilot recipient to be given the award whilst not on active duty. Katajainen ran a small business for a number of years immediately after the war, before joining the Helsinki City legal department and retiring in 1982 as a distrainer. Katajainen died on 16 January 1997 at the age of 78.

## 1st Lieutenant Lauri Vilhelm Nissinen

Lauri 'Lapra' Nissinen was born in Joensuu, in eastern Finland, on 31 July 1918. In 1936 he volunteered for military service at LAs. 3, becoming a mechanic, an in 1938 he was accepted into the ISK and was posted to LLv 24 as a sergeant pilot on 1 March 1939, flying D.XXIs. During the Winter War he was a member of the 3rd Flight, scoring four bomber kills

3/LeLv 24's Sgt Nils Katajainen sits astride the tailplane of Brewster BW-368 on 26 September 1941 – the day he scored his sixth kill, achieved in this very aircraft (*Katajainen*)

in FR-98. At the end of the conflict he had 'made' master sergeant.

Nissinen was still with 3/LeLv 24, now flying Brewsters, come 25 June 1941, and he used his first assigned fighter (BW-353) to score 'double' kills in his first two combats on 7 and 7 July. Two months later he was given BW-384, which he duly took with him to 2/LeLv 24, in eastern Karelia, on 21 January 1942. Nissinen aspired to become an officer, and following completion of several courses, he 'made' reserve 2nd lieutenant on 30 March 1942, although cadet school had to wait a while.

On 6 April Nissinen claimed three Hurricanes in BW-384, and he continued to use this fighter until 8 June 1942, when he scored his 20th kill of the Continuation War. This qualified him for the Mannerheim Cross (No 69), which he received on 5 July – four days after he had started cadet school. On 26

1/HLeLv 24 leader, 1Lt Lauri Nissinen, climbs out of a Bf 109G on 4 April 1944 (*V Lakio*)

March 1943 he graduated as a 1st lieutenant, and was made CO of 1/LeLv 24 (still flying Brewsters) on 21 June.

In April 1944 Nissinen's unit converted to Bf 109Gs, and he was assigned MT-225. He had claimed six victories with the fighter up to 17 June 1944 when he was killed in MT-229 – Nissinen had commenced a diving attack on Il-2s with his wingman, 2Lt Heimo Lampi, when his fighter was suddenly hit from above by the remains of MT-227, flown by 12.5-kill ace 1Lt Urho Sarjamo, which had had its starboard wing shot off. Nissinen had flown around 300 sorties and had scored 32.5 kills.

## 1st Lieutenant Kyösti Keijo Ensio Karhila

Kyösti Karhila was born on 2 May 1921 in Rauma, in south-western Finland. In 1939 he volunteered for military service and was accepted into the ISK, where he became a fighter pilot. On 18 March 1941 2Lt Karhila was assigned to 1/LLv 32, flying firstly D.XXIs and then Curtiss Hawks from mid-July onwards. On 19 September he scored his fifth kill (a MiG-3) in CUw-560 to thus become an ace at just 20 years of age.

'Kössi' Karhila kept on claiming victories until 20 April 1943 when he was posted to LeLv 34, equipped with Bf 109Gs, following his promotion to 1st lieutenant. His tally then stood at 13, all scored in Hawks. Part of to the 2nd Flight, Karhila made an immediate impact in MT-214 by claiming a 'double' on 4 May 1943, and he kept on steadily scoring until 22 August 1943, when his flight moved to Helsinki-Malmi on city defence duties. On 6 March 1944 he was transferred to HLeLv 30, before returning to HLeLv 34 on 15 June.

3/HLeLv 24 leader, 1Lt Kyösti Karhila is seen on 2 July 1944 (*SA-kuva*)

On 30 June he assumed command of 3/HLeLv 24 following the the serious wounding of Hans Wind – this promotion was quite unusual, for the post of flight leader usually belonged to a regular officer. He duly was assigned MT-461 (one of the 'gun boat' G-6/R6s), and used it to score eight kills. On 21 July Karhila was promoted to command 2/HLeLv 30, but by that late stage in the war the action was all but over. He had flown some 304 sorties and claimed 32 victories.

On 14 November 1944 he resigned from the service and became an air traffic controller for a year, before becoming an airline pilot, captain and finally an inspector before officially retiring in 1973. Thereafter he flew charter airliners and business jets until 1985 when he finally retired for good. Karhila is still alive and well at the time of writing.

## Major Jorma Karhunen

Karhunen was born on 17 March 1913 at Pyhäjärvi, in southern Finland. In 1933 he graduated from secondary school and joined up for military service, entering the ISK. In 1936 he graduated from the cadet school and was posted as a junior flying officer to *Lentoasema* 1, which duly became *Lentorykmentti* 2 on 1 January 1938.

HLeLv 31 (ex-HLeLv 24) commander, Maj Jorma Karhunen, is seen in 1945 (*I Juutilainen*)

At the outbreak of the Winter War 1Lt Karhunen was the deputy leader of 1/LLv 24, flying D.XXIs. He was assigned FR-112, and he used this fighter to score most of his 4.5 victories up to 30 January 1940, when he took over 2/LLv 24. He failed to add to his score following his new posting as he spent the rest of the Winter War in Sweden performing evaluation flights and pilot training on the then new Brewster Model 239.

When hostilities resumed on 25 June 1941 'Joppe' Karhunen was leading 3/LeLv 24 in his personal Brewster, BW-366, which he flew for two years. He became an ace in his first combat of the new conflict on 4 July 1941 by down an SB. Exactly a month later he was promoted to captain, and he continued to lead his flight into 1942, scoring 'double' kills on three occasions – 26 September, 17 December and 26 February.

During the first great air battles over the Gulf of Finland in the summer of 1942, Karhunen's flight benefited greatly from his leadership. Indeed, during the week commencing 12 August 3/LeLv 24 downed 25 aircraft, Karhunen himself (flying BW-38) scoring two 'triples' on the 16th and 18th. On 8 September he was decorated with the Mannerheim Cross (No 92) for both his outstanding leadership and personal tally of 25 kills.

Karhunen kept on scoring until 4 May 1943 when he downed an I-153 for his 31st, and last, victory. On 1 June he was appointed commander of *Lentolaivue* 24, and three months later was promoted to major – he had flown 350 missions prior to be promoted out of the frontline.

After the war Karhunen remained in active service, being promoted to lieutenant-colonel on 6 December 1951 and given command of *Lentorykmentti* 1 (which had become 2. Lennosto within a year), based at Pori.

Karhunen finally retired from active duty on 13 December 1955, and in 1967 he was promoted to full colonel in reserve. He commenced a career as a writer soon after leaving the air force, publishing works detailing both his own wartime experiences and those of his fellow fighter pilots. Karhunen has written over 30 books during the past four decades, plus in excess of 200 magazine articles. He is still alive and well today.

# APPENDICES

## Ace Listing

| Rank | Name | Squadron | Victories Total | Victories by type | | | | | | |
|---|---|---|---|---|---|---|---|---|---|---|
| | | | | FR | GL | FA | MS | BW | CU | MT |
| WO | Juutilainen, Ilmari** | 24, 34 | 94 | 2 | | | | 34 | | 58 |
| Capt | Wind, Hans** | 24 | 75 | | | | | 39 | | 36 |
| Maj | Luukkanen, Eino* | 24, 34 | 56 | 2.5 | | | | 14.5 | | 39 |
| WO | Lehtovaara, Urho* | 28, 34 | 44.5 | | | | 15 | | | 29.5 |
| WO | Tuominen, Oiva* | 26, 34 | 44 | 1.5 | 6.5 | 23 | | | | 13 |
| Capt | Puhakka, Olli* | 26, 34 | 42 | 4 | | 13 | | | | 25 |
| 1Lt | Puro, Olavi | 6, 24 | 36[1] | | | | | 5.5 | | 28.5 |
| MSgt | Katajainen, Nils* | 24 | 35.5 | | | | | 17.5 | | 18 |
| 1Lt | Nissinen, Lauri*+ | 24 | 32.5 | 4 | | | | 22.5 | | 6 |
| 1Lt | Karhila, Kyösti | 32, 30, 34, 24 | 32 | | | | | | 13 | 19 |
| Capt | Karhunen, Jorma* | 24 | 31 | 4.5 | | | | 26.5 | | |
| MSgt | Vesa, Emil | 24 | 29.5 | | | | | 9.5 | | 20 |
| SSgt | Järvi, Tapio | 24 | 28.5 | | | | | 11.5 | | 17 |
| SSgt | Alakoski, Klaus | 26, 34 | 26 | | | 1 | | | | 25 |
| 1Lt | Tervo, Kalevi+ | 24, 32, 34 | 23 | | | | | 0.5 | 15.5 | 7 |
| 1Lt | Saarinen, Jorma+ | 24 | 23 | | | | | 5 | | 18 |
| WO | Kinnunen, Eero+ | 24 | 22.5 | 3.5 | | | | 19 | | |
| MSgt | Tani, Antti | 28, 34 | 21.5 | | | | 7 | | | 14.5 |
| 1Lt | Myllylä, Paavo | 28, 34 | 21 | | | | 1.5 | | | 19.5 |
| 1Lt | Suhonen, Väinö | 24 | 19.5 | | | | | 4.5 | | 15 |
| WO | Pyötsiä, Viktor | 24 | 19.5 | 7.5 | | | | 8.5 | | 3.5 |
| 1Lt | Teromaa, Erik | 24, 26 | 19 | | | | | 13 | | 6 |
| Capt | Pekuri, Lauri# | 24, 34 | 18.5 | | | | | 12.5 | | 6 |
| MSgt | Huotari, Jouko | 24 | 17.5 | | | | | 9.5 | | 8 |
| WO | Turkka, Yrjö | 24, 34 | 17 | 4.5 | | | | 9.5 | | 3 |
| Capt | Sarvanto, Jorma | 24 | 17 | 13 | | | | 4 | | |
| 1Lt | Lumme, Aulis | 24 | 16.5 | | | | | 11.5 | | 5 |
| 1Lt | Riihikallio, Eero | 24 | 16.5 | | | | | 6.5 | | 10 |
| Sgt | Halonen, Eero | 24 | 16 | | | | | | | 16 |
| MSgt | Alho, Martti## | 24 | 15 | 1.5 | | | | 13.5 | | |
| SSgt | Nuorala, Aaro | 30, 14, 34 | 14.5 | 3 | | | 1.5 | | | 10 |
| 2Lt | Lampi, Heimo | 24 | 13.5 | | | | | 5.5 | | 8 |
| 1Lt | Kokko, Pekka## | 24 | 13.5 | 3.5 | | | | 10 | | |
| 2Lt | Pallasvuo, Yrjö+ | 32, 34 | 13 | | | | | | 9 | 4 |
| Capt | Sovelius, Per-Erik | 24 | 12.5 | 5.5 | | | | 7 | | |
| MSgt | Aaltonen, Lasse | 26, 34 | 12.5 | 2 | | 3.5 | | | | 7 |
| 1Lt | Sarjamo, Urho+ | 24 | 12.5 | | | | | 6.5 | | 6 |
| MSgt | Paronen, Onni | 26, 34 | 12.5 | 2 | | 5.5 | | | | 5 |
| WO | Koskinen, Eino | 32 | 12.5[2] | | | | | | 11.5 | |
| SSgt | Ahokas, Leo | 24 | 12 | | | | | 7 | | 5 |
| Capt | Törrönen, Iikka+ | 24 | 11 | 0.5 | | | | 10.5 | | |
| Capt | Nieminen, Urho | 26 | 11 | 5 | | 4 | | 2 | | |
| SSgt | Leino, Hemmo | 30, 14, 34 | 11 | 1.5 | | 3 | | | | 6.5 |
| SSgt | Erkinheimo, Niilo## | 32, 34 | 10.5 | | | | | | 6.5 | 4 |
| Capt | Kalima, Martti | 30, 10, 14 | 10.5 | 4 | | 6.5 | | | | |
| 1Lt | Metsola, Kai | 24 | 10.5 | | | | | 6.5 | | 4 |
| SSgt | Peltola, Eino+ | 24, 34 | 10.5 | | | | | 7.5 | | 3 |
| Capt | Lahtela, Kullervo | 32, 34 | 10.5 | | | | | | 6 | 4.5 |

| Rank | Name | Squadron | Victories Total | Victories by type | | | | | | |
|---|---|---|---|---|---|---|---|---|---|---|
| | | | | FR | GL | FA | MS | BW | CU | MT |
| Capt | Karu, Veikko* | 26, 28, 30 | 10 | 7 | | | 2 | 1 | | |
| 1Lt | Laitinen, Ahti# | 24 | 10 | | | | | 2 | | 8 |
| 1Lt | Pasila, Mikko | 24 | 10 | | | | | 5 | | 5 |
| 2Lt | Kirjonen, Mauno | 32, 34 | 10 | 1 | | | | | 5 | 4 |
| Capt | Berg, Paavo+ | 26, 32 | 9.5 | | 5 | | | | 4.5 | |
| SSgt | Kauppinen, Viljo | 24 | 9.5 | | | | | 8.5 | | 1 |
| 1Lt | Hillo, Jaakko | 32 | 8 | | | | | | 8 | |
| 1Lt | Mattila, Ture | 30, 34 | 8 | 3 | | | | | | 5 |
| 1Lt | Savonen, Joel | 24 | 8 | | | | | 7 | | 1 |
| 2Lt | Inehmo, Martti+ | 28 | 8 | | | | 8 | | | |
| SSgt | Lyly, Erik | 24, 34 | 8 | | | | | 2 | | 6 |
| Capt | Bremer, Aulis | 32 | 8 | | | | | | 8 | |
| WO | Porvari, Valio | 26 | 7.5[3] | | 2 | 3.5 | | 1 | | |
| MSgt | Jutila, Lauri+ | 32, 34 | 7.5 | | | | | | 4 | 3.5 |
| 1Lt | Trontti, Nils | 26 | 7 | | | 6 | | 1 | | |
| Sgt | Virtanen, Väinö | 32 | 7 | | | | | | 7 | |
| Sgt | Tomminen, Toivo+ | 28 | 6.5 | | | | 6.5 | | | |
| 1Lt | Huhanantti, Tatu+ | 24 | 6 | 6 | | | | | | |
| 2Lt | Linnamaa, Aarre+ | 28 | 6 | | | | 6 | | | |
| MSgt | Salminen, Pauli | 32 | 6 | 0.5 | | | | | 5.5 | |
| SSgt | Virta, Kelpo## | 24 | 6 | 6 | | | | | | |
| Sgt | Avikainen, Onni | 24 | 6 | | | | | 6 | | |
| SSgt | Hattinen, Lars | 28 | 6[4] | | | | 6 | | | |
| Sgt | Durchman, Matti | 34 | 6 | | | | | | | 6 |
| Capt | Nurminen, Pentti# | 32 | 6 | | | | | | 6 | |
| SSgt | Gerdt, Aimo | 32 | 6 | | | | | | 6 | |
| MSgt | Ikonen, Sakari | 24 | 6 | 2 | | | | 4 | | |
| Maj | Magnusson, Gustaf* | 24 | 5.5 | 4 | | | | 1.5 | | |
| 1Lt | Kauppinen, Osmo | 24 | 5.5 | | | | | 5.5 | | |
| WO | Lautamäki, Lauri | 26 | 5.5 | | 1.5 | 4 | | | | |
| WO | Fräntilä, Mauno | 24, 32, 34 | 5.5 | 1 | | | | | 1.5 | 3 |
| Sgt | Keskinummi, Kosti | 24 | 5.5 | | | | | 0.5 | | 5 |
| Sgt | Mellin, Paavo# | 24 | 5.5 | | | | | 5.5 | | |
| WO | Rimminen, Veikko | 24 | 5.5 | 1.5 | | | | 4 | | |
| Sgt | Kiljunen, Aaro | 32 | 5.5 | | | | | | 5.5 | |
| SSgt | Tilli, Pentti+ | 24 | 5 | 5 | | | | | | |
| Maj | Ehrnrooth, Olavi## | Koel, 32 | 5[5] | 1 | | 2 | | | 2 | |
| Capt | Myllymäki, Jouko+ | 28, 24 | 5 | | | | 2 | | | 3 |
| 1Lt | Alapuro, Sakari | 32 | 5 | | | | | | 5 | |
| 1Lt | Evinen, Veikko+ | 32, 34 | 5 | 2.5 | | | | | 1.5 | 1 |
| 1Lt | Lakio, Vilppu | 24 | 5 | | | | | 5 | | |
| 1Lt | Lindberg, Kim | 24 | 5 | | | | | 5 | | |
| 1Lt | Massinen, Pauli | 28 | 5 | | | | 5 | | | |
| 1Lt | Nyman, Atte | 24 | 5 | | | | | | | 5 |
| 1Lt | Pokela, Väinö | 24, 34 | 5 | | | | | 2 | | 3 |
| SSgt | Kajanto, Jaakko+ | 32 | 5 | | | | | 5 | | |
| Sgt | Koskelainen, Arvo | 24 | 5 | | | | | | 5 | |
| Sgt | Joensuu, Ilmari | 26 | 5 | | 4 | 1 | | | | |

**See overleaf for notes to this listing**

**Notes** (for victories listing on previous pages)

(1)     Two victories with I-153
(2)     One victory with LaGG-3
(3)     One victory with Bulldog
(4)     Three victories with Mörkö Morane
(5)     Three victories as a test pilot

**         Double Mannerheim Cross winner
*          Mannerheim Cross winner
+          Killed or missing in action
#          Prisoner of War
##        Killed in flying accident

- The rank stated is the one held at the time of the last victory
- Only those units are mentioned where victories were scored
- The shared victories are rounded to the nearest half

## Unit Histories

The basic Finnish fighter unit was a *Lentolaivue* (a squadron). Its theoretical strength was 27 aircraft, divided into three eight-fighter flights. However, due to the vagaries of aircraft availability, a squadron could muster up as many as 35 fighters, or as few as six. A typical 'alert' flight consisted of a four-fighter *Schwarm*. By the summer of 1944 a squadron would rarely have more than a flight airborne at any one time, although bomber escort missions usually required two flights to fulfil the mission requirements.

*Lentolaivue* was abbreviated to LLv up to May 1942, when it was changed to LeLv. For the sake of clarity, the latter designation is used throughout this volume for the Continuation War. On 14 February 1944 all frontline units received an operational prefix, with fighter squadrons becoming *Hävittäjälentolaivues*, which was duly abbreviated to HLeLv.

### *Lentolaivue* 24 - *Hävittäjälentolaivue* 24

**Commanders:** Capt (Lt-Col) Gustaf Magnusson from November 1938, and Capt (Maj) Jorma Karhunen from June 1943

**Equipment:** Fokker D.XXI (Mercury) in April 1938, Brewster Model 239 in April 1940 and Messerschmitt Bf 109G in April 1944

*Lentolaivue* 24 was founded on 15 July 1933 following a major re-organisation of the air force which saw 'air stations' formed and flying units duly subordinated to them. *Lentoasema* 1 (LAs 1), controlling LLv 10 and 24 at Utti, became known as the 'cradle of fighter pilots', and on 1 January 1938 the 'air stations' were transformed into 'flying regiments', with LAs 1 becoming LeR 2.

At the outbreak of the Winter War on 30 November 1939, LLv 24 was based at Immola with 35

D.XXIs split between five flights – two of these had actually been seconded to the squadron from LLv 26. On 28 December 1939 the headquarters moved to Joutseno, and the squadron was split into detachments to be used wherever it was deemed necessary. On 25 February 1940 the unit returned temporarily to Immola, before moving to Lemi on 1 March and then Ristiina ten days later. The Winter War ended on 13 March 1940.

The following month saw LLv 24 transferred to Joroinen, where it exchanged its Fokkers with LLv 32 for Brewster Model 239s. In August the newly-built Vesivehmaa airfield welcomed the unit for a period of intensive training.

The start of the Continuation War on 25 June 1941 saw LLv 24 (flying 33 Brewsters split between four flights) become part of LeR 2 and move to Vesivehmaa. On 2 July the bulk of the squadron was sent to Rantasalmi, whilst smaller detachments operated from various bases. By 16 September the majority of LLv 24 had regrouped at the 'dry shore' bases of Lunkula or Mantsi. On 23 December the bulk of the unit moved closer to the front by flying into Kontupohja 'ice base', although it pulled back to Hirvas come the warmer spring weather on 14 April 1942.

On 18 July LLv 24 was transferred to LeR 3, and two weeks late the headquarters and three flights moved to Römpötti. By 21 November the unit had assembled at Suulajärvi, on the Karelian Isthmus. On 11 February 1943 attrition forced LeLv 24 to reduce its flight numbers to three, each assigned eight Brewsters.

On 14 February 1944 the unit was redesignated *Hävittäjälentolaivue* 24 (Fighter Squadron 24), and two months later the first Bf 109G-2s were received, allowing the surviving Brewsters to be passed on to HLeLv 26 in May.

In early June the squadron came under sustained Soviet attack at Suulajärvi, forcing HLeLv 24 to retreat firstly to Immola on 11 June, followed four days later by a move to Lappeenranta, which ultimately proved to be its last wartime base. On 4 September 1944 the Continuation War ended, and exactly three months later all Finnish squadrons were re-numbered, HLeLv 24 becoming HLeLv 31.

*Hävittäjälentolaivue* 24 claimed 877 aerial victories during both wars – 96 in D.XXIs, 477 in Brewsters and 304 with the Bf 109G. In return it lost 55 aircraft to all causes, 44 of which fell in combat – 11 D.XXIs, 19 Brewsters and 14 Bf 109Gs. Some 27 of its pilots were either killed or posted missing, and a further three became POWs. Finally, the unit produced five Mannerheim Cross winners.

### *Lentolaivue* 26 - *Hävittäjälentolaivue* 26

**Commanders:** Capt Erkki Heinilä February from 1939, Maj Raoul Harju-Jeanty from December 1939, Capt (Maj) Eino Carlsson from December 1941, Maj Lauri Larjo from March 1944 and Maj Erkki Metsola from July 1944

**Equipment:** Bulldog IV from July 1935, Gladiator II from January 1940, Fiat G.50 from February 1940 and Brewster Model 239 from May 1944

Formed on 15 July 1933 and assigned to *Lentoasema* 5, *Lentolaivue* 26 transferred to LeR 2 on 1 January 1938 when all fighter squadrons were concentrated into one regiment.

30 November 1939 found the squadron based at Heinjoki with just ten Bulldogs, for its two D.XXI-equipped flights had been temporarily transferred to LLv 24, which was serving near to the frontline. The Bulldog flight, meanwhile, was restricted to patrolling areas where it was less likely that they would come across superior Soviet fighters. Finally, on 2 February 1940 the veteran Bristol biplane fighters were handed over to training units.

The Bulldog was partially replaced by the ultimate British biplane fighter, the Gladiator. On 19 January LLv 26 had received the first of its Gloster fighters, which would eventually re-equip two flights, plus Fiat G.50s for the third. The former were flown from various bases until the end of February 1940, when they were handed over to LeR 1. The rest of the Winter War was fought with the Fiats from Utti and, from 15 February onwards, Haukkajärvi. In July LLv 26 moved to Joroinen.

When the Continuation War broke out on 25 June 1941, LLv 26 (still assigned to LeR 2 at Joroinen) could field 26 G.50s split between three flights. On 6 July the unit's headquarters moved to Joensuu, with subordinate flights using various bases until 2 August, when the squadron came together again at Lunkula.

On 13 September the unit was transferred to LeR 3 and sent to Immola, with detachments flying from several bases. On 5 July 1942 LeLv 26 went to Kilpasilta, on the Karelian Isthmus, and on 14 February 1944 became *Hävittäjälentolaivue* 26.

On 9 May 1944 it moved to Heinjoki, from where its veteran Fiats were finally sent to training units following the arrival of marginally younger Brewster Model 239s – these were received in two batches from HLeLv 24. Based some way away from the renewed Red Army assault of mid-1944, the squadron moved on 14 June to Immola and then to Käkisalmi 48 hours later. On 7 July HLeLv 26 was again transferred, this time to Mensuvaara, before moving to Värtsila 19 days later. Here, it became part of LeR 2 on 4 August 1944.

The end of the Continuation War resulted in the unit moving to Onttola on 8 September, and then to Vaala on 2 October 1944. From here a flight of Brewsters, joined by Myrskys from TLeLv 12, participated in the Lapland War against the Germans.

On 18 October the outfit was stationed at Kemi and on 4 December it became HLeLv 23. On 23 January 1945 the unit was transferred to Rissala, which was its designated peace-time base.

*Hävittäjälentolaivue* 26 claimed 183 aerial victories during the three wars in which it participated – six in Bulldogs, 25 in D.XXIs, 34 in Gladiators, 99 in G.50s

and 19 with Brewsters. In turn it lost 41 aircraft to all causes, 28 of which were downed in action, and 16 pilots were either killed or posted missing. Finally, the first air force Mannerheim Cross winner emerged from this unit.

## Lentolaivue 28 - Hävittäjälentolaivue 28

**Commanders:** Maj Niilo Jusu from December 1939, Capt (Maj) Sven-Erik Siren from May 1941, Maj Auvo Maunula from August 1942 and Maj Per-Erik Sovelius from June 1944

**Equipment:** Morane-Saulnier MS.406 from February 1940 and Mörkö Morane (M-105) and Messerschmitt Bf 109G from July 1944

*Lentolaivue* 28 was established at Utti on 8 December 1939 as part of LeR 2. During February 1940 30 MS.406s were received and issued to three flights, the unit then moving to Säkylä, in south-western Finland. Two of these flights later flew from Hollola during the final stages of the Winter War, which ended on 13 March.

During the truce the squadron was transferred to Naarajärvi, where it remained until the commencement of the Continuation War – it consisted of 27 MS.406s, split between three flights, at the time. Still controlled by LeR 2, LLv 28 moved to Joroinen on 4 July 1941, and then to Joensuu two weeks later. By 29 July, the squadron was back at Joroinen, however, although it moved closer to the action on 19 August when it flew into Karkunranta 'dry shore base'. On 18 October the squadron returned to 'solid land' when it was posted back to Viitana – from here it sent out small detachments to various bases.

On 3 August 1942 the headquarters and the bulk of LeLv 28 moved to Hirvas. Following air force-wide redesignations on 14 February 1944, the unit became *Hävittäjälentolaivue* 28.

In the wake of the Soviet offensive, 'Detachment Sovelius' was formed on 10 June 1944, its two flights being controlled by LeR 3 at Lappeenranta. In late June 1944 the detachment received Bf 109Gs, allowing it to hand over its Moranes to the 1st flight, which also began converting to Mörkö Moranes at the same time. On 11 July the squadron flew to Värtsilä, where 'Detachment Sovelius' merged back into HLeLv 28 within 12 days of the parent unit's arrival. The squadron remained a part of LeR 2.

Following the ceasefire, HLeLv 28 saw further action with its Mörkö Moranes in the briefly fought Lapland War, together with an MS.406 flight from of TLeLv 14. Initially based at Paltamo on 2 October 1944, the unit moved to Kemi just two weeks later. On 27 November 1944 all flights returned to Rissala, thus marking the end of the war for them. On 4 December the unit became *Hävittäjälentolaivue* 21.

During two wars *Hävittäjälentolaivue* 28 had claimed 133 aircraft shot down – 118 for the MS.406 and 15 for the Bf 109G. It had lost 39 aircraft to all causes, with 26 (all MS.406s) destroyed during combat and had 18 pilots killed or posted missing in action, plus a further three made PoWs.

## Lentolaivue 30 - Hävittäjälentolaivue 30

**Commanders:** Capt (Maj) Lauri Bremer from April 1940, Maj Olavi Seeve from May 1942, Maj Eino Luukkanen from November 1942, Capt (Maj) Toivo Kivilahti from March 1943, Maj Arvo Hassinen from November 1943 and Capt (Maj) Veikko Karu from May 1944

**Equipment:** Fokker D.XXI (Wasp) from March 1941, Polikarpov I-153 from November 1942 and Messerschmitt Bf 109G from February 1944

When *Lentorykmentti* 3 was established on 27 March 1940, *Lentolaivue* 30 was also created to act as an advanced training squadron for the group. A year later it was transformed into a frontline fighter squadron, and by 25 June 1941 it had five Hurricanes and 18 D.XXIs on strength, split between three flights, at Pori. On 1 July the Hurricane flight was handed over to LLv 32, and two days later the rest of the squadron moved to Hyvinkää, with detachments being sent to various local bases. On 1 September the unit flew to Utti, and 17 days later the 3rd Flight moved south to Viena to form the nucleus of LLv 10. On 21 October the remaining 25 D.XXIs split into a two-flight squadron based at Suulajärvi.

LLv 10 disbanded on 1 November 1941, although its 3rd Flight remained active until merged with LeLv 14 14 on 1 August 1942. On 16 November 1942 LeLv 30 became a reconnaissance unit following its transfer to LeR 5, its D.XXIs being exchanged for captured I-153s and the unit moved ted to Römpötti.

On 14 February 1944 it was renamed *Hävittäjälentolaivue* 30 and transformed into a fighter squadron once again. It subsequently operated two flights of Bf 109Gs primarily from Vesivehmaa (detachments flew from other bases as well) until war's end.

*Hävittäjälentolaivue* 30 claimed 39 aerial victories – 36 in D.XXIs and three in Bf 109Gs. Some 24 aircraft were in turn lost to all cause, eight of which were the result of combat (six D.XXIs, one I-153 and two Bf 109Gs). Eleven pilots were killed. The Mannerheim Cross was awarded to a solitary pilot from the unit.

## Lentolaivue 32 - Hävittäjälentolaivue 32

**Commanders:** Capt Erkki Heinilä from April 1940, Maj Olavi Ehrnrooth from July 1941, Maj Lauri Bremer from January 1943 and Capt (Maj) Kullervo Lahtela from June 1944

**Equipment:** Fokker D.XXI (Mercury) from April 1940 and Curtiss Hawk 75A from July 1941

On 27 March 1940 LeR 2's LLv 22 was transferred to LeR 3 and re-designated LLv 32. The following month it exchanged its Brewsters with LLv 24, receiving D.XXIs in their place, and then moved to Siikakangas. With the outbreak of the Continuation War, the squadron flew its 25 D.XXIs (split between three flights) to Hyvinkää, and on 1 July it was joined by a Hurricane flight from LLv 30. Within ten days the squadron had arrived at Utti to start its conversion onto Curtiss Hawks, duly receiving 15 aircraft in three flights by 1 August – it then moved to Lappeenranta. On 17 August the Hurricane detachment flew south to Viena, and LLv 32 was itself eventually replaced by LLv 10 on 23 September 1941 when the former unit was transferred to Suuläjärvi.

On 3 May 1942 LeR 1 was established, and it was soon given control of LLv 32. The unit had been sent to Nurmoila, on the Olonets Isthmus, by the end of the month. On 14 February 1944 the unit was re-named *Hävittäjälentolaivue* 32.

Following the Russian onslaught in the Olonets in June, HLeLv 32 fled firstly to Uomaa and then to Mensuvaara on 4 July, where it remained until war's end. On 4 December 1944 the unit was disbanded.

*Hävittäjälentolaivue* 32 claimed 202 aircraft shot down – five in D.XXIs, six in Hurricanes, 190 in Hawks and one with the LaGG-3. It lost 29 aircraft in return, 18 of them in action – two D.XXIs, one Hurricane and 15 Hawks. Sixteen pilots were killed or posted missing in action, and a further two became PoWs.

## Lentolaivue 34 - Hävittäjälentolaivue 34

**Commanders:** Maj Olavi Ehrnrooth from January 1943 and Maj Eino Luukkanen from March 1943

**Equipment:** Messerschmitt Bf 109G from March 1943

LeLv 34 was established on 23 January 1943 as part of LeR 3. Between March and May 1943 30 Bf 109Gs arrived as its equipment, the unit being based at Utti, with smaller detachments flying from other sites. On 2 August the squadron moved to Kymi.

On 14 February 1944 the unit became *Hävittäjälen-tilaivue* 34, and two days later the whole of the 2nd Flight was handed over to HLeLv 30. Thereafter, the unit fought through to war's end with just two flights of Bf 109Gs.

Following the major Soviet attack on 9 June 1944, HLeLv 34 moved firstly to Immola three days later, and then again to Lappeenranta on 16 June. Finally, on 23 June it was transferred to Taipalsaari, which became its last wartime base. On 4 December 1944 the unit was re-numbered HLeLv 33.

*Hävittäjälentolaivue* 34 claimed 345 kills, all with the Bf 109G, and of the 30 fighters lost to all cause, 18 were downed in combat. Twelve pilots were either killed or posted missing and one became a PoW. Finally, three of its aces were awarded the Mannerheim Cross.

# Speed and Climbing Performance of Finnish Fighters*

| Top speed in kmh: | D.XXI | D.XXI | MS.406 | G.50 | B-239 | H 75A-6 | Bf 109G-2 |
|---|---|---|---|---|---|---|---|
| 0 m | 355 | 342 | 372 | 372 | 428 | 400 | 523 |
| 1000 m | 369 | 351 | 386 | 383 | 439 | 417 | 547 |
| 2000 m | 383 | 360 | 400 | 396 | 448 | 424 | 575 |
| 3000 m | 397 | 354 | 408 | 408 | 443 | 432 | 589 |
| 4000 m | 407 | 346 | 415 | 417 | 461 | 426 | 596 |
| 5000 m | 412 | 335 | 440 | 418 | 480 | 416 | 610 |
| 6000 m | 413 | 320 | 440 | 406 | 469 | 407 | 639 |

| Climb to: | D.XXI | D.XXI | MS.406 | G.50 | B-239 | H 75A-6 | Bf 109G-2 |
|---|---|---|---|---|---|---|---|
| 1000 m | 1 m 10 s | 1 m 45 s | 1 m 55 s | 1 m 10 s | 1 m 27 s | 1 m 25 s | 0 m 45 s |
| 2000 m | 2 m 20 s | 3 m 30 s | 3 m 50 s | 2 m 50 s | 2 m 30 s | 2 m 45 s | 1 m 25 s |
| 3000 m | 3 m 30 s | 5 m 25 s | 5 m 30 s | 4 m 10 s | 4 m 12 s | 4 m 10 s | 2 m 20 s |
| 4000 m | 4 m 40 s | 7 m 40 s | 7 m 35 s | 6 m 15 s | 5 m 35 s | 5 m 50 s | 3 m 15 s |
| 5000 m | 6 m 10 s | 10 m 30 s | 10 m 00 s | 8 m 00 s | 7 m 10 s | 8 m 00 s | 4 m 10 s |
| 6000 m | 8 m 00 s | 15 m 15 s | 13 m 20 s | 10 m 20 s | 9 s 15 m | 11 m 00 s | 5 m 05 s |

| | D.XXI | D.XXI | MS.406 | G.50 | B-239 | H 75A-6 | Bf 109G-2 |
|---|---|---|---|---|---|---|---|
| **Flown by:** | FR-107 | FR-143 | MS-311 | FA-15 | BW-366 | CU-557 | MT-215 |
| **Flown on:** | 11/11/39 | 17/5/41 | 22/8/42 | 16/6/42 | 20/5/40 | 6/7/41 | 5/4/43 |
| **Engine:** | 840 hp Mercury | 825 hp R-1535 | 860 hp 12Y31 | 840 hp A.74 | 950 hp R-1820 | 1065 hp R-1830 | 1475 hp DB 605A |
| **Armament:** fuselage: | 2 x 7.7 mm | | 1 x 12.7 mm | 2 x 12.7 mm | 1 x 12.7 mm 1 x 7.7 mm | 2 x 7.5 mm | 1 x 20 mm 2x7.92 mm |
| wing: | 2 x 7.7 mm | 4 x 7.7 mm | 2 x 7.5 mm | | 2 x 12.7 mm | 2 x 7.5 mm | |

*All aircraft were flown in loaded condition, with full fuel tanks, gun magazines and no external stores

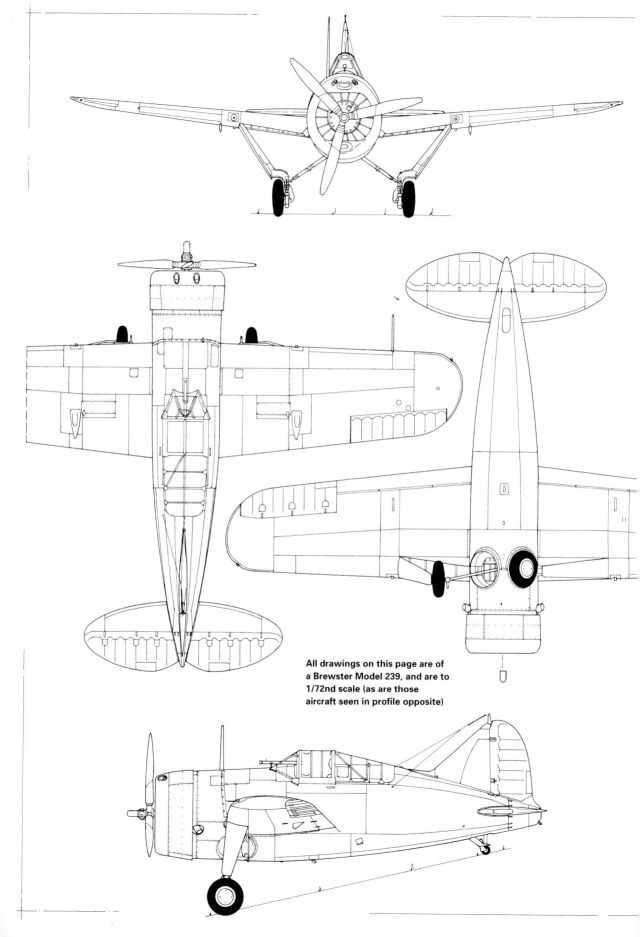

All drawings on this page are of
a Brewster Model 239, and are to
1/72nd scale (as are those
aircraft seen in profile opposite)

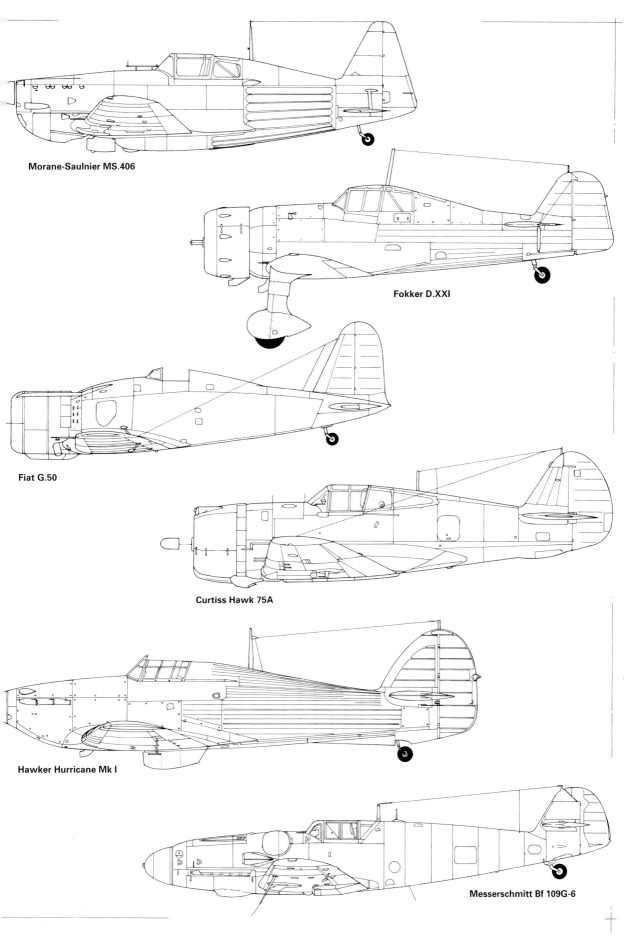

Morane-Saulnier MS.406

Fokker D.XXI

Fiat G.50

Curtiss Hawk 75A

Hawker Hurricane Mk I

Messerschmitt Bf 109G-6

# COLOUR PLATES

## 1

**Bulldog IVA BU-68 of Sgt Valio Porvari, Os. Heinilä/LLv 26, Heinjoki, December 1939**

During the October 1939 war exercises, this aircraft was assigned to Sgt Porvari. Less than two months later, during the Finnish Air Force's first encounters with Soviet aircraft on 1 December, the same fighter/pilot combination claimed an SB, which was duly credited as a probable. On Christmas Day Porvari used this Bulldog to gain a confirmed victory in the shape of an I-16 over the Karelian Isthmus. 'Valtsu' Porvari's 'big day' came on 25 June 1941 when he was credited with 3.5 SBs destroyed whilst flying Fiat G.50 FA-20 – a month later he was promoted to warrant officer. Porvari served throughout the war with LeLv 26, finishing with a tally of 7.5 kills from 251 sorties

## 2

**Gladiator II GL-256 of Cpl Ilmari Joensuu, 2/LLv 26, Ruokolahti, February 1940**

'Pitkä-Jim' ('Long Jim') Joensuu was assigned to LLv 26 on 26 January 1940, and within a month of his arrival he had been credited with four confirmed victories, all while flying this machine. He became an ace on 13 August 1941 when he downed a 'Chaika' flying LLv 26 G.50 FA-35. Joensuu was then posted to cadet school to become a regular officer, but he failed to add to his tally upon joining the Bf 109G-equipped HLeLv 34 during the summer of 1944.

## 3

**Fiat G.50 (MM 4738) SA-1 of Capt Olavi Ehrnrooth, CO of KoeL, Tampere, January 1940**

SA-1 (later FA-1) was the first G.50 to arrive to Finland on 18 December 1939. It remained with the *Koelentue* (air force test unit) at the State Aircraft Factory at Tampere for evaluation purposes for some time, and whilst here Capt Ehrnrooth flew it on several interception missions, claiming two bombers. From 12 July 1941 Ehrnrooth commanded the Hawk-equipped LeLv 32, and he scored his fifth, and last, victory on 28 March 1942. On 19 January 1943 Ehrnrooth was posted to command the new Bf 109G unit LeLv 34, but on 27 March 1943 was killed in a flying accident.

## 4

**Morane-Saulnier MS.406 MS-318/'Yellow 3' of 2Lt Pauli Massinen, 3/LLv 28, Säkylä, February 1940**

Massinen joined 2/LLv 28 when it was formed on 8 December 1939. On 2 March 1940 he downed a DB-3M in this aircraft, the star on the rudder denoting the kill. Massinen continued to serve as a first lieutenant with 2/LeLv 28 into 1941, becoming an ace on 21 August 1941 flying MS-314. He claimed five kills in 40 sorties, before being posted to the air fighting school as an instructor on 7 November 1941. Massinen remained in this post through to the end of the war.

## 5

**Fokker D.XXI (c/n III/11) FR-110/'Blue 7' of WO Viktor Pyötsiä, 3/LLv 24, Joroinen, April 1940**

Serving with 3/LLv 24, Pyötsiä scored 7.5 kills during the Winter War with FR-110, this score including two 'doubles' on 27 December 1939 and 20 January 1940. This fighter is one of only two known examples to have carried victory symbols during the Winter War. 'Isä-Vikki' ('Father-Vikki') was one of the 'old hands' of LLv 24, remaining with the unit throughout the five years of conflict. Aside from his success with the D.XXI, he also scored kills in Brewsters and Bf 109Gs, which took his accumulated total to 19.5 kills in 437 sorties (the latter figure being the second highest total for any Finnish fighter pilot). On 3 July 1944 he was shot down in Bf 109G MT-235, but he successfully parachuted to safety.

## 6

**Fokker D.XXI (c/n III/1) FR-97/'White 2' of 1Lt Jorma Sarvanto, 4/LLv 24, Utti, January 1940**

Sarvanto became the first Finnish ace during a four-minute action on 6 January 1940, using this aircraft to down six DB-3Ms of 6.DBAP south of Utti. This action received much coverage in the global press, and 'Zamba' Sarvanto went on to score a total of 13 kills in the Winter War. He later added a further four victories in Brewsters again with LeLv 24. After flying a total of 251 sorties, Sarvanto became an instructor in the final months of the Continuation War, using his skills to train future fighter pilots.

## 7

**Fokker D.XXI (c/n III/13) FR-112/'Black 7' of 1Lt Jorma Karhunen, 1/LLv 24, Immola, December 1939**

'Joppe' Karhunen flew FR-112 for five weeks whilst deputy leader of 1/LLv 24, scoring three and two shared kills during this time. His scoring run in the fighter came to an end on 3 January 1940 when FR-112 was damaged in a taxiing accident with another D.XXI at Värtsilä, causing it to be sent away for repairs – his final score with the Fokker fighter was 4.5. On 30 January Karhunen was appointed commander of 2/LLv 24, although he spent the rest of the Winter War test flying Brewsters in Sweden (see rear cover profile caption).

## 8

**Fokker D.XXI (c/n III/3) FR-99/'Black 1' of Maj Gustaf Magnusson, CO of LLv 24, Joutseno, January 1940**

'Eka' Magnusson assumed command of LLv 24 a year before the Winter War broke out. A firm believer in the four-fighter unit, he imparted his beliefs with determination to all his pilots, and this duly led to his squadron having a clear tactical advantage over its Soviet counterparts, resulting in a great number of aerial victories being scored. Magnusson downed four bombers during the Winter War, and achieved 'acedom' whilst still in command of LLv 24 on 8 July 1941 when he claimed a DB-3M in Brewster BW-380. From May 1943 he commanded LeR 3, creating an indigenous early warning and fighter control system (without radar) which played a key role in repelling the Soviet summer offensive of 1944. On 26 June 1944 he won the Mannerheim Cross for these achievements.

## 9

**Morane-Saulnier MS.406 (No 674) MS-622/'Red 2' of Capt Martti Kalima, CO of 2/TLeLv 14, Tiiksjärvi, June 1944**

'Masa' Kalima took command of 2/TLeLv 14 on 25 October 1943, and was assigned this fighter some five months later. He used it to gain the last four of his 10.5 victories, scored during the course of 285 sorties. Earlier in the Continuation War, Kalima had flown D.XXIs with LeLv 30 and 10, downing four Soviet aircraft. On 1 August 1942 he had transferred to 1/LeLv 14, where he had initially flown MS-326, before being issued with this fighter. On 16 June 1944 he was placed in charge of a detachment sent to Germany for nightfighter training, but returned to Finland following the ceasefire on 4 September 1944.

## 10
**Fiat G.50 (MM 3614) FA-25/'Yellow 1' of Capt Olli Puhakka, CO of 3/LeLv 26, Kilpasilta, December 1942**
Deputy leader of 3/LeLv 26 from the beginning of the Continuation War, Puhakka used G.50 FA-1 to down six kills. On 10 June 1942 he was given command of 3/LeLv 26 and issued with FA-25, downing five aircraft in it. By the time he swapped from a G.50 to a Bf 109G (see caption for profile 39) in February 1943, Puhakka had scored 13 kills with the type.

## 11
**Fiat G.50 (MM 4736) FA-15/'Yellow 5' of Sgt Klaus Alakoski, 3/LeLv 26, Kilpasilta, November 1942**
'Santtu' Alakoski joined LeLv 26 on 7 July 1941, and he made only one kill in the G.50, on 13 August 1941. On 7 November 1942 Alakoski joined 3/LeLv 26, where he was was assigned FA-15 until 16 April 1943, when he was posted to 3/LeLv 34. He enjoyed far more success with the Bf 109G, however, steadily building up his score to 26 in 239 sorties.

## 12
**Polikarpov I-153 IT-18/'Grey 8' of 2Lt Olavi Puro, 3/LeLv 6, Römpötti, November 1942**
On 25 September 1942 'Olli' Puro was posted to 3/LeLv 3 to fly captured I-153s, and on 4 October he claimed a 'Chaika' and on 12 November a Pe-2 – both while flying this aircraft. On 4 April 1943 he was transferred to 2/LeLv 24, where he scored a further 5.5 kills in Brewsters. The Soviet Offensive of June 1944 offered Puro further opportunities to add to his tally, and by the end of the campaign he had downed 28.5 aircraft in Bf 109Gs out of a total of 36 (from 207 sorties).

## 13
**Morane-Saulnier MS.406 MS-327/'White 9' of SSgt Urho Lehtovaara, 2/LeLv 28, Viitana, November 1941**
With 15 victories to his credit in MS.406s, 'Pikku-Jätti' ('Little Giant') Urho Lehtovaara was the leading Morane ace of the Finnish Air Force. Beginning his career with LLv 28 on 10 February 1940, he had flown MS-327 during the early months of the Continuation War until it suffered a start up fire on 23 December. On 28 March 1943 he was posted to 3/LeLv 34 to fly Bf 109Gs, and he went on to score 29.5 kills in the German fighter. On 9 July 1944 Lehtovaara was awarded the Mannerheim Cross after passing the 40-victory mark.

## 14
**Morane-Saulnier MS.406 MS-317/'Black 2' of 1Lt Paavo Myllylä, 1/LeLv 28, Äänislinna, July 1942**
Myllylä was a Winter War veteran with both LLv 26 and 28, having joined the latter unit on 6 February 1940. On 1 September 1941 he was assigned MS-317 as a member of 1/LeLv 28, and 'Pampsa' Myllylä duly scored 1.5 kills with it

until posted to 3/LeLv 34 on 9 February 1943. He remained with the latter unit until war's end, by which time he had flown 420 sorties and claimed 21 kills. The markings on the leading edge of MS-317's fin denote all the kills scored by pilots flying this aircraft.

## 15
**Fiat G.50 (MM 4743) FA-26/'White 5' of WO Oiva Tuominen, 1/LeLv 26, Kilpasilta, October 1942**
Already an eight-victory ace from the Winter War, 'Oippa' Tuominen went on to become the top scoring G.50 pilot during the Continuation War. He flew with 1/LeLv 26 and was assigned FA-26 until 8 February 1943, when he was posted to LeLv 34. Tuominen scored 13 of his 23 Fiat kills in this fighter, and on 18 August 1941 he became the first air force Mannerheim Cross winner after passing the 20-kill mark. He added a further 13 victories in Bf 109Gs, raising his final tally to 44 aircraft destroyed in 400+ sorties.

## 16
**Fokker D.XXI (c/n IV/12) FR-129/'Red 1' of Capt Veikko Karu, CO of 2/LeLv 30, Suulajärvi, November 1941**
Karu scored three kills in the Winter War and built up an impressive record whilst leading 2/LeLv 30 on mainly anti-shipping duties during the first 18 months of the Continuation War. He used this Twin Wasp Jnr-powered D.XXI to score half of his final tally of ten confirmed victories, which included four flying boats – his flight also sunk 17 light surface vessels in the Gulf of Finland. On 6 November 1942 Karu was awarded the Mannerheim Cross, after which he performed staff tours before being given command of the Bf 109G-equipped HLeLv 30 on 22 May 1944. He failed to add to his score, however.

## 17
**Brewster Model 239 BW-384/'Orange 3' of 2Lt Lauri Nissinen, 2/LeLv 24, Tiiksjärvi, May 1942**
MSgt 'Lapra' Nissinen initially saw action in the Continuation War flying Brewsters with 3/LeLv 24 – he was assigned BW-384 on 12 August 1941. On 28 January 1942 Nissinen was transferred to 2/LeLv 24 and sent to southern Viena to fight an ever increasing number of lend-lease Hurricanes flying out of Murmansk. On 8 June 1942 he scored his 20th kill of the Continuation War in BW-384, this tally including six Hurricanes. He was was decorated with the Mannerheim Cross on 5 July 1942 (see caption for profile 33).

## 18
**Brewster Model 239 BW-352/'White 2' of MSgt Eero Kinnunen, 2/LeLv 24, Tiiksjärvi, September 1942**
'Lekkeri' Kinnunen scored 3.5 kills in the Winter War in D.XXI FR-109. Flying Brewster BW-352 by the outbreak of the Continuation War, he used this fighter during one of the first encounters of the conflict on 25 June 1941, the action in question seeing five SBs destroyed.. Kinnunen shared the kills on this occasion with Cpl Heimo Lampi, and he scored a further two during his next mission. Kinnunen flew BW-352 throughout his career, firstly with 2/LeLv 24 and, from 11 February 1943, 3/LeLv 24. On 21 April 1943 WO Kinnunen was downed by Oranienbaum anti-aircraft fire, crashing to his death in this machine. His had scored 22.5 kills.

## 19

**Brewster Model 239 BW-393/'White 7' of 1Lt Hans Wind, CO of 1/LeLv 24, Suulajärvi, January 1943**

Young 1Lt 'Hasse' Wind joined 4/LLv 24 on 1 August 1941, and it took him eight months to become an ace – his fifth kill took the form of a shared victory on 29 March 1942 in BW-378. The following August he was posted to the 1/LeLv 24, and his score quickly started to escalate whilst flying BW-393. On 10 November Wind took command of the flight, and by the time he was made CO of 3/LeLv 24 on 27 May 1943, the fin of BW-393 showed 29 kills (see caption for profile 23).

## 20

**Brewster Model 239 BW-377/'Black 1' of SSgt Tapio Järvi, 4/LeLv 24, Römpötti, October 1942**

"Tappi" ('Shorty') Järvi was a member of LeLv 24 from 11 August 1941 until war's end. On 11 February 1943 his flight merged into 2/LeLv 24, and it was here that he scored most of his kills – Järvi used BW-377 to claim 7.5 aircraft destroyed. During the 1944 offensive, he flew mostly wing-cannon armed Bf 109G-6/R6 MT-450, claiming ten Il-2s with it. By the time he 'made' master sergeant on 16 July 1944, Järvi's scoring run had come to an end, finishing on 28.5 in 247 sorties.

## 21

**Brewster Model 239 BW-390/'White 0' of 2Lt Kai Metsola, 1/LeLv 24, Nurmoila, October 1941**

Metsola served in 1/LeLv 24 throughout the Continuation War, being assigned BW-390 early on in the campaign – he eventually claimed three kills with it. On 2 February 1942 he was promoted to first lieutenant, which was the highest rank a pilot in reserve (non-cadet graduate) could reach. From April 1944 he flew Bf 109Gs (usually MT-231), and by war's end he had downed 10.5 kills during the course of 296 sorties.

## 22

**Brewster Model 239 BW-364/'Orange 4' of WO Ilmari Juutilainen, 3/LeLv 24, Suulajärvi, December 1942**

BW-364 was assigned to 3/LeLv 24's 'Illu' Juutilainen from June 1941 to February 1943, during which time he scored an amazing 28 victories with it. The fin markings shows his score of two in D.XXIs and 34 in Brewsters up to this point. On 26 April 1942 Juutilainen won the Mannerheim Cross for his 20 kills in the Continuation War, and on 8 February 1943 he was posted to the newly-formed Bf 109G-equipped LeLv 34, joining the 1st Flight (see caption for profile 30).

## 23

**Brewster Model 239 BW-393/'Orange 9' of Capt Hans Wind, CO of 3/LeLv 24, Suulajärvi, April 1944**

When Wind assumed command of 3/LeLv 24 on 27 May 1943, he took BW-393 with him, its tactical tail number being changed to 'Orange 9' so as to mirror the flight's assigned markings. On 31 July 1943 he was awarded the Mannerheim Cross. Of Wind's 39 Brewster victories, 26 were claimed in BW-393, which he flew until April 1944, when his squadron converted to Bf 109Gs. MT-201 and MT-439 proved to be the most successful of his new mounts, and he added a further 36 kills (25 in ten days) to take his tally to 75 in 302 sorties. Wounded in action on 28 June, Wind received a second Mannerheim Cross whilst in hospital recuperating.

## 24

**Brewster Model 239 BW-370/'Black 4' of 1Lt Aulis Lumme, 4/LeLv 24, Römpötti, October 1942**

Joining LeLv 24 at the beginning of the Continuation War, Lumme was one of the few reserve pilots appointed to lead a flight – he commanded 2/LeLv 24 twice following the loss of its regular CO, remaining in charge until a replacement officer was found. Lumme flew BW-370 for two years, firstly with 4/LeLv 24 and then from 11 February 1943 with 2/LeLv 24, during which time he claimed 4.5 kills with it. The machine later received the squadron's lynx emblem on its forward fuselage. By the end of hostilities Lumme had flown 287 sorties and scored 16.5 confirmed aerial victories.

## 25

**Hurricane I (N2394) HC452/'Black 2' of SSgt Lauri Jutila, LeLv 32, Suulajärvi, May 1942**

*Lentolaivue* 32 flew a handful of Hurricanes for 12 months commencing 1 July 1941, scoring six victories with the type in that time. Jutila was one of the assigned pilots for HC452, although he failed to claim any kills with it.. He had achieved a total of 7.5 victories whilst flying Hawks and Bf 109Gs (the latter with LeLv 34) by the time he was shot down and killed by return fire from an Il-4 bomber on 17 June 1943. The Ilyushin later crashed as a result of the damage Jutila had inflicted upon it prior to being fatally hit whilst flying MT-214.

## 26

**Curtiss Hawk 75A-6 (c/n 13644) CUw-560/'Yellow 0' of 2Lt Kyösti Karhila, 1/LeLv 32, Lappeenranta, September 1941**

Part of 1/LeLv 32 since the beginning of the Continuation War 'Kössi' Karhila regularly flew CUw-560 (the 'w' stood for Twin Wasp engine, although this was deleted following a major repair or overhaul). He scored eight victories in CUw-560, and by the time he transferred to LeLv 34 (see caption for profile 35) on 20 April 1943, he had 13 aircraft to his credit. LeLv 32, unlike other units, did not assign specific aircraft to its pilots.

## 27

**Curtiss Hawk 75A-3 (c/n 13747) CU-552/'White 2' of 2Lt Kalevi Tervo, 2/LeLv 32, Nurmoila, June 1942**

Tervo was the ranking Finnish Hawk pilot with a score of 15.5 victories. After a brief tour with LeLv 24, 'Kale' Tervo was posted on 8 April 1942 to 2/LeLv 32, where he flew CU-552 on many missions, scoring six kills. On 11 February 1943 Tervo joined 1/LeLv 34, being one of the top scoring aces hand picked to man the new unit.. On 20 August he was posted missing in action in Bf 109G-2 MT-219, his fighter having almost certainly been downed by Lavansaari's notorious flak batteries. Tervo's score then stood at 23, six of these having been claimed in Bf 109Gs.

## 28

**Curtiss Hawk 75A-2 (No 170) CU-581/'Blue 1' of Capt Veikko Evinen, CO of 3/HLeLv 32, Nurmoila, March 1944**

Evinen took command of 3/HLeLv 32 on 20 February 1944, being assigned CU-581. On 24 June he was leading his flight in this aircraft on a strafing mission against the Soviet invasion fleet on Lake Ladoga when his fighter received hits and crashed at Tuulos – Evinen died of his wounds the following

day. His score of five kills was achieved flying D.XXIs and
Hawks with LeLv 32, and Bf 109Gs with LeLv 34.

## 29
### Bf 109G-2 (Wk-Nr 14718) MT-201/'White 1' of Maj Eino Luukkanen, CO of LeLv 34, Utti, June 1943
By the time he assumed command of LeLv 34 on 29 March
1943, 'Eikka' Luukkanen had 2.5 D.XXI victories from the
Winter War (leading 3/LLv 24) and 14.5 kills in Brewsters (CO
of 1/LeLv 24) to his credit. Flying MT-201 for a year,
Luukkanen claimed nine aircraft shot down. His score rapidly
increased following the Soviet offensive of mid-1944, the ace
using MT-417 and MT-415 to down 25 aircraft in just a matter
of weeks. On 5 August he claimed his 56th, and last, victory
in the form of a Yak-9 over the Gulf of Finland. Aside from finishing third in the aces' listing, Luukkanen also completed a
staggering 441 sorties. On 18 June 1944 he was awarded the
Mannerheim Cross for a sustained period of outstanding leadership.

## 30
### Bf 109G-2 (Wk-Nr 14753) MT-212/'Red 2' of WO Ilmari Juutilainen, 1/LeLv 34, Utti, May 1943
MT-212 was assigned to Juutilainen on 13 March 1943, and
11 days later he scored the first Finnish Messerschmitt victory (a Pe-2) with it. On 2 June Tuominen ditched the fighter
after hitting debris from a Pe-2 he had just shot down.
Juutilainen's later mounts were MT-222 (see cover illustra-
tion), MT-426 and MT-457, and he finished as the top Finnish
ace on the Bf 109G with 58 victories. On 28 June 1944 he
received his second Mannerheim Cross, being one of only
four Finnish soldiers to 'do the double'. 'Illu' Juutilainen flew
437 missions and claimed 94 victories, ranking him top
amongst non-German European fighter aces.

## 31
### Bf 109G-6/R6 (Wk-Nr 165249) MT-477/'Yellow 7' of 1Lt Mikko Pasila, 1/HLeLv 24, Lappeenranta, July 1944
MT-477 was one of 14 'Kanonenboote' delivered to Finland,
although the aircraft's standard armament of one 20 mm cannon and two 13 mm machine-guns was found to be more
than adequate, as the Finns were used to firing at very short
distances. The bulky 20 mm wing cannon were therefore
removed from most 'gun boats', MT-477 being no exception
– Pasila flew this fighter during the final two months of hostilities. Belonging to 1/LeLv 24 from 17 December 1941 until
war's end, Pasila scored ten victories; five apiece in
Brewsters and Bf 109Gs, although none of the latter came
whilst flying this particular fighter.

## 32
### Bf 109G-6 (Wk-Nr 165001) MT-460/'Yellow 8' of SSgt Emil Vesa, 3/HLeLv 24, Lappeenranta, July 1944
Vesa served with 3/LeLv 24 from 3 December 1941 to war's
end. He scored 9.5 kills with Brewsters before transitioning to
Bf 109Gs in April 1944. During the Soviet assault of mid-1944,
Vesa flew MT-438 until he was forced to belly-land it after suffering combat damage on 28 June 1944. He was then issued
with MT-460, and went on to claim eight kills with the G-6
between 30 June and 19 July. Vesa flew 198 sorties and
claimed 29.5 victories.

## 33
### Bf 109G-2 (Wk-Nr 13577) MT-225/'Yellow 5' of 1Lt Lauri Nissinen, CO of 1/HLeLv 24, Suulajärvi, May 1944
After graduating from cadet school, 'Lapra' Nissinen (see cap-
tion for profile 17) led 1/LeLv 24 from 8 July 1943. On 4 April
1944 MT-225 was assigned to him, although he failed to
score any kills with it before a wounded SSgt Viljo Kauppinen
(9.5 kills) wrote it off after crash-landing following combat on
7 June 1944. On 17 June the remains of MT-227 (minus its
right wing, which had been shot off), flown by 12.5-kill ace
1Lt Urho Sarjamo, crashed into Nissinen in MT-229 as the latter commenced a diving attack on Soviet aircraft , killing both
pilots – Nissinen was the only Mannerheim Cross winner lost
in action. His score at the time of his death stood at 32.5 aircraft destroyed.

## 34
### Bf 109G-6 (Wk-Nr 412122) MT-423/'White 3' of SSgt Hemmo Leino, 1/HLeLv 34, Kymi, June 1944
Leino scored 11 victories in 251 missions, flying D.XXIs with
3/LeLv 30, MS.406s with 1/LeLv 14 and Bf 109Gs with
1/HLeLv 34 – he was posted to the latter unit on 19 April
1943. A year later he was assigned MT-423, which had
arrived directly on the squadron following its construction in
Germany. The new unit emblem (derived from an idea put forward by its commanding officer), comprising a fledgling eagle,
was painted onto the rudder of this fighter and MT-451 in
May 1944, these being the only known wartime applications
of the badge.

## 35
### Bf 109G-6/R6 (Wk-Nr 165342) MT-461/'Yellow 6' of 1Lt Kyösti Karhila, CO of 3/HLeLv 24, Lappeenranta, July 1944
After two years with LeLv 32, 'Kössi' Karhila (see caption for
profile 26) was posted to 2/LeLv 34 on 20 April 1943 to fly Bf
109Gs. As an officer in the reserve, Karhila replaced the
wounded Wind at the head of 3/HLeLv 24 on 28 June 1944.
MT-461 was then his assigned fighter, and he chose to keep
its wing cannon, claiming eight aircraft with the 'gun boat'. He
scored his last kill on 18 July 1944, taking his tally to 32 victories in 304 sorties.

## 36
### Bf 109G-6 (Wk-Nr 411901) MT-428/'White 8' of MSgt Antti Tani, 1/HLeLv 34, Lappeenranta, June 1944
Tani joined LLv 28 on 13 February 1940 and duly became one
of its leading MS.406 aces with seven victories whilst with
the 1st Flight. On 15 April 1943 he was posted to 3/LeLv 34,
which was equipped with Bf 109Gs, and on 6 March 1944 he
scored a 'triple' flying MT-209. Three months later Tani was
transferred to 1/HLeLv 34 and assigned MT-428, which he
used to score two kills. On 1 July Tani again achieved a 'triple'
haul flying G-6/R6 MT-453. He ended the war with 21.5 kills
from 272 sorties.

## 37
### Bf 109G-2 (Wk-Nr 14754) MT-213/'White 3' of 1Lt Eero Riihikallio, 2/HLeLv 24, Suulajärvi, May 1944
Riihikallio was posted to 2/LeLv 24 just prior to Christmas
1941, and it took him 11 months to make his first kill – a

Tomahawk on 23 November 1942 flying BW-377. Within six months his score had risen to 6.5, however. During the Soviet summer offensive of 1944 he flew MT-213, which is seen devoid of the tactical number '3' following the introduction of a new numbering system on 22 May 1944. Despite flying just 110 sorties, Riihikallio claimed 16.5 victories (three of which were scored in MT-213).

## 38

**Bf 109G-6 (Wk-Nr 166007) MT-487/'Yellow 7' of WO Mauno Fräntilä, 2/HLeLv 30, Kymi, August 1944**

MT-487 arrived to Finland on 23 July 1944 and was issued to 2/HLeLv 30. Two weeks later it was assigned to 'Manu' Fräntilä, who had scored his first kill as long ago as the Winter War in a D.XXI from LLv 24. He added a further 1.5 kills in Hawks with LeLv 32 in 1942, before being posted to LeLv 34 on 9 February 1943 to fly Bf 109Gs. On 20 August 1943 he successfully bailed out of MT-224 after it had burst into flames whilst in flight. Fräntilä eventually flew 380 sorties and was credited with 5.5 victories, three of which came in Bf 109Gs, although none in MT-487.

## 39

**Bf 109G-6 (Wk-Nr 164943) MT-433/'Yellow 3' of Capt Olli Puhakka, CO of 3/HLeLv 34, Taipalsaari, August 1944**

Olli Puhakka (see caption for profile 10) took command of 3/LeLv 34 on 9 February 1943, and was assigned MT-204 a month later. He flew it for a year before converting with the rest of his squadron to the G-6, and being issued with MT-419. On 17 June 1944 the fighter was shot up in combat, forcing Puhakka to perform a belly-landing. Its replacement was MT-433, which arrived two days later. The ace downed 42 aircraft (including two in this fighter – a P-39 on 28 June and a Pe-2 24 hours later) during 402 sorties, and on 21 December 1944 he was awarded the Mannerheim Cross.

## 40

**Bf 109G-6 (Wk-Nr 165461) MT-476/'Yellow 7' of MSgt Nils Katajainen, 3/HLeLv 24, Lappeenranta, July 1944**

As a member of 3/LeLv 24, Katajainen had become an ace on Brewsters on 12 August 1941. By the time he converted to the Bf 109G in April 1944 his tally had risen to 17.5, and over the next three months he quickly added a further 18 kills. However, on 5 July Katajainen was wounded in combat soon after downing a Yak-9, forcing him to crash-land MT-476 at Lappeenranta. During the course of 196 sorties he accounted for 35.5 kills, and was duly awarded the Mannerheim Cross on 21 December 1944 – the only non-active-duty fighter pilot to receive the honour.

## Rear cover

**Brewster Model 239 BW-366/'Orange 6' of Capt Jorma Karhunen, CO of 3/LeLv 24, Suulajärvi, May 1943**

BW-366 was assigned to Karhunen from the start of the Continuation War on 25 June 1941, and he claimed his 31st, and last, kill in this machine on 4 May 1943 – an I-153 over the Gulf of Finland. He led 3/LeLv 24 until 27 May 1943, when he was given command of the whole squadron. By this stage 'Joppe' Karhunen had received the Mannerheim Cross (on 8 September 1942) for both his outstanding leadership qualities and impressive personal score.

# FIGURE PLATES

## 1

SSgt Nils Katajainen of 3/LeLv 24 at Suulajärvi in May 1943 is wearing the standard woollen m/36 service dress, including cap and boots. This uniform was worn throughout the ranks, except in the navy. At the bottom of his left chest pocket is his pilot's badge, issued in this form between 1916 and 1944. Katajainen's rank is shown on the collar patches, whilst his epaulettes bear the air arm symbol.

## 2

WO Viktor Pyötsiä of 3/LLv 24 at Värtsilä in January 1940 is wearing the standard m/36 dress uniform of the Finnish Air Force beneath his winter flying overall. The latter was a must in order to fend off temperatures of -30°C. His leather helmet and goggles are of Finnish design, whilst his hands are kept warm through the wearing of dog skin mittens, which have only the thumb and forefinger separated to allow him to grip objects. Completing his winter garb, Pyötsiä has felt boots on his feet.

## 3

Capt Aulis Bremer, CO of 2/LeLv 32 at Suulajärvi in April 1942. He too is wearing m/36 service dress beneath his own leather jacket, which has his rank stripes sewn on to the left arm only. Over the jacket is worn an m/27 waistbelt, plus a thinner cross-strap issued exclusively to officers and warrant officers, in addition to the pistol holster belt. Bremer's peaked cap is a standard m/27 item issued to all personnel, although his laced boots and woollen socks are private purchase items.

## 4

1Lt Hans Wind, CO of 3/LeLv 24 at Suulajärvi in August 1943. He is wearing standard air force officer's m/27 service dress, with rank stripes on both sleeves and epaulettes bearing the air force and Finnish state lion emblems. Above his left pocket is the awards stripe, whilst on the pocket itself is the Mannerheim Cross. Beneath the latter is Wind's pilot's badge, and to the right of both is his Cadet corps emblem. Finally, the ribbon through the first button hole of his tunic denotes his awarding of the German Iron Cross, 2nd class.

## 5

1Lt Kyösti Karhila, CO of 3/HLeLv 24 at Lappeenranta in July 1944. He is attired in standard German fighter pilot's jacket, pocket trousers, life vest and lightweight cloth helmet. This equipment was bought directly from Germany from early 1943 onwards primarily for the Bf 109G pilots. Indeed, only Karhila's boots are standard Finnish Air Force items.

## 6

WO Ilmari Juutilainen of 1/HLeLv 34 at Taipalsaari in July 1944. He is wearing an m/39 summer blouse with m/27 waistbelt and cross-strap, air force issue m/27 trousers and standard issue boots. The summer cap is also an air force m/22 model, whilst the neck scarf was a favourite of the ranking Finnish ace. The rank insignia on the collar patches were unique to the air force's warrant officers. The left chest pocket is adorned with Juutilainen's Mannerheim Cross, and immediately below the decoration is his pilot's badge. Note also the Fokker and Messerschmitt manufacturers' pins fastened to his cross-strap.